Old Sheffield

Paul Chrystal

Birdseye view of Sheffield.

Stenlake Publishing Ltd

Text © Paul Chrystal, 2022.
First published in the United Kingdom, 2022,
by Stenlake Publishing Ltd.,
54-58 Mill Square,
Catrine,
KA5 6RD

01290 551122
www.stenlake.co.uk

ISBN 978-1-84033-891-1

The publishers regret that they cannot supply copies of any pictures featured in this book.

Printed by
Blissetts, Unit E1-E8 Shield Drive,
West Cross Ind Pk, Brentford, TW8 9EX

Acknowledgements

I take a responsible attitude to copyright and, where appropriate, endeavour to obtain permission from the rights holders for use of their images, photographs and/or photographs on their websites or in publications. Absence of contact details or response means that this is not always possible so you are encouraged to contact me if you require accreditation for the use of any photograph, or to request its removal. Other images are believed to be in the public domain. A number of individuals and organisations have been helpful in granting permission to use information and images in this book. They include Chris Taylor, Sales and Marketing Director, Swann-Morton Limited; Tony Lax, Great Northern Books; and Chris Hobbs, c.g.hobbs@sheffield.ac.uk, for information relating to Nunnery Colliery available on his superb website.

The stream, Whiteley Woods, Sheffield.

Introduction

At Creswell Crags to the east of the city is the first historical evidence of human activity and occupation in the Sheffield area: during the Iron Age the region was in the southernmost part of the territory of the Brigantes, that troublesome tribe which caused many a problem for the Romans in the early days following their invasion of our shores in 43 BC. When the Romans finally left Britannia to its own devices and defences, around AD 410, the Sheffield area probably formed the southern part of the Brittonic kingdom of Elmet, with the Rivers Sheaf (hence Sheffield) and Don forming part of the boundary between Elmet and the Kingdom of Mercia while Anglian settlers pushed west from the Kingdom of Deira. Evidence of a Britonnic presence around Sheffield comes with two settlements called Wales and Waleswood. However, the settlements that grew and merged to form the Sheffield we know, date from the second half of the first millennium, and are of Anglo-Saxon and Danish origin. In Anglo-Saxon times, the Sheffield region straddled the border between the kingdoms of Mercia and Northumbria. The *Anglo-Saxon Chronicle* tells how Eanred of Northumbria submitted to Egbert of Wessex at the hamlet of Dore, now a suburb of Sheffield, in 829.

The Norman Conquest came and went: one of the consequences was that Sheffield Castle was built to protect the locality from native incursions, and a small town sprang up which forms the nucleus of the modern city. By 1296 a market had been established at what is now Castle Square leading Sheffield to grow into a small market town. Industry – specifically steel, cutlery and coal – has always been vital to Sheffield.

Sheffield Manor Lodge, also known as Sheffield Manor or Manor Castle, is a lodge built about 1516 in what then was a large deer park southeast of Sheffield, to provide a country retreat for George Talbot, the 4th Earl of Shrewsbury and his family. What remains of this estate is now known as Norfolk Park. The remains of the Lodge include parts of the kitchens, long gallery, and the Grade II* listed Turret House, also called "Queen Mary's Tower", which has fine 16th-century ceilings. Mary, Queen of Scots, was held prisoner here by the 6th Earl of Shrewsbury at both Sheffield Manor Lodge and Sheffield Castle. Two of Mary's letters are preserved in the Sheffield Archives. In 1582, while Mary was still being held at Sheffield, an illuminating inventory of all the household goods and furniture belonging to George, Earl of Shrewsbury was made. Included in the inventory is the "stuff" of the "Queen of Scots and her people". The list of rooms for "her people" includes those of the Master of the "quences howsholde", a Mr Burgon as her doctor and a Mr Jarvys as her "surgion".

The Industrial Revolution was the making of Sheffield but it had its downsides – not least the exploitation of workers – men, women and children – in the workplace and hideous living conditions which, apart from anything else, contributed to the deaths of 402 residents in the 1832 cholera epidemic. The population of the town continued to grow rapidly throughout the 19th century, increasing from 60,095 in 1801 to 451,195 by 1901 and adding to the public health and social problems endemic to the city.

The coming of the railways was a major game-changer for all sorts of reasons. The Sheffield and Rotherham Railway opened in 1838, connecting the two towns. Sheffield was incorporated as a borough in 1842, and was granted a city charter in 1893. The continual influx of people led to a need and demand for better water supplies, so a number of new reservoirs were constructed on the outskirts of the town. The catastrophic collapse of the dam wall of one of these reservoirs in 1864 resulted in the 'Great Sheffield Flood', which drowned 270 people and wrecked large areas of the city. Eighty years later Sheffield's steel factories were repurposed to manufacture armaments and ammunition thus making the city an obvious target for the Luftwaffe: the nights of 12th and 15th December 1940 – the Sheffield Blitz – were particularly horrendous with more than 660 lives lost and many industrial and commercial buildings and much housing stock destroyed.

Sheffield's *Women of Steel* – an award-winning bronze sculpture that commemorates the dignified and inspirational women of Sheffield who worked in the city's steel industry during the World Wars.

John Walsh's bombed out department store on George Street.

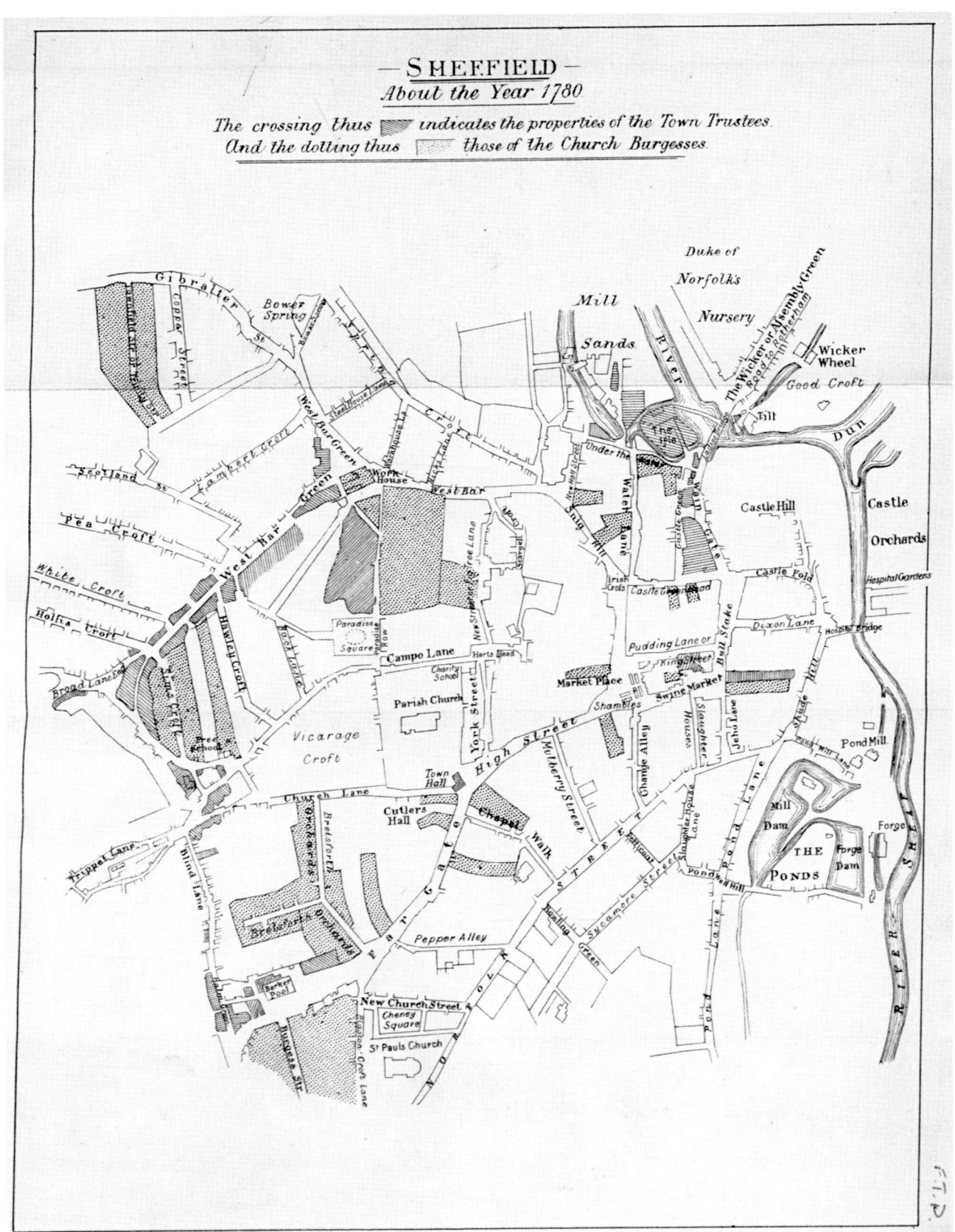

Sheffield in 1780.
From the *Records of the Burgery of Sheffield Commonly Called the Town Trust* (London 1897).

Industry

It is easy just to describe Sheffield before the 1970s as a city defined by its industry – and indeed steel, specifically cutlery, and coal had dominated the economy and society of the city for 200 years or so, but Sheffield's entire area is given over to green space, and a third of the city lies within the beautiful Peak District National Park. Sheffield can boast more than 250 parks, woodlands and gardens which are home to around 4.5 million trees.

In the 13th century, Sheffield had already earned a reputation for the production of knives, as referenced in Geoffrey Chaucer's *The Canterbury Tales* (1297):

"Ther was no man, for peril, dorste hym touche. A Sheffeld thwitel baar he in his hose. Round was his face, and camus was his nose".

- Geoffrey Chaucer, *Reeve's Tale*.

Indeed, by the early 1600s it was the epicentre of English cutlery manufacture outside London, regulated by the Company of Cutlers in Hallamshire. Sheffield took a leading role in the Industrial Revolution and can point to making and developing many significant inventions and new technologies. The 19th century saw a massive expansion of its traditional cutlery trade when stainless steel and crucible steel were developed locally, fuelling an almost tenfold increase in the population. Sheffield became known as "Steel City"; after Benjamin Huntsman discovered the crucible technique in the 1740s at his workshop in Handsworth leading to the production of much higher quality steel. This was rendered obsolete in 1856 when Henry Bessemer made the Bessemer converter.

Thomas Boulsover of Sheffield's Cutlers Company invented Sheffield Plate in 1743, invented that is by accident: he was trying to repair the handle of a customer's decorative knife; but heated it too much and the silver started to melt. When he examined the damaged handle he noticed that the silver and copper had fused together; the two metals behaved as one when he tried to reshape them, even though he could clearly see the two layers. Boulsover saw an opportunity and set up in business, funded by Strelley Pegge of Beauchief, and carried out further experiments in which he put a thin sheet of silver on a thick ingot of copper and heated the two together to fuse them. When the composite block was hammered or rolled to make it thinner, the two metals were reduced in thickness at similar rates. Using this method, Boulsover was able to make sheets of metal which had a thin layer of silver on the top surface and a thick layer of copper underneath. When this new material was used to make buttons, they looked and behaved like silver buttons but were obviously a fraction of the cost. The "double sandwich" form of Sheffield plate was developed around 1770. Used for items such as bowls and mugs that had a visible interior, it consisted of a sheet of silver each side of a piece of copper; early manufacturers applied a film of solder over the bare edge of copper.

Stainless steel was invented by Harry Brearley in 1912, bringing affordable cutlery to your tea table. The work of F. B. Pickering and T. Gladman throughout the 1960s, 1970s and 1980s was fundamental to the development of modern high-strength low-alloy steels.

Sadly it was not to last, for international competition in iron and steel led to a decline in these industries in the 1970s and 1980s, coinciding with the collapse of coal mining in the region.

A Sheffield buffer girl. Buffing was the main occupation of women metal trades workers in Sheffield, where women used the brown paper made from old rope and designed for product wrapping to protect themselves from flying 'muck', making aprons with it and wrapping it around their legs and feet.

South East View of Sheffield, William Ibbitt (1854), now in Sheffield City Museums. The agrarian scenes in the foreground elide into an industrial landscape of Satanic industrialisation replete with belching chimneys and pitheads. Also depicted are canal staithes and barges, workmen on break and washday women. (Creative Commons Attribution 4.0 licence.)

Men with their crucible steel making tools. Crucible steel is steel made by melting pig iron (cast iron), iron, and sometimes steel, often along with sand, glass, ashes, and other fluxes, in a crucible.

William Jessop & Sons advertisement from about 1875 showing Park Works in Sheffield (top), their Manchester warehouse (left) and the Soho Mills, Sheffield (right). Thomas Jessop was born on 30th January 1804 at the family home in Blast Lane; later he was to be both mayor and master cutler. Expanding markets in the United States led to Jessop and his brothers joining the business in 1830. In January 1844 the business relocated to a site in the Brightside area. Later a works at Kilnhurst was added. The extensive Brightside Works covered 30 acres; on the deaths of his father and brothers, Thomas took sole charge of the business in 1871. By 1876 all work had moved to the Brightside site, then known as Brightside Steel Works, and said to be in the 1880s the largest manufacturer of steel in the Sheffield area.

Grace's Guide describes Jessop in 1914 as Steel manufacturers. Specialities: high-grade crucible steel for every purpose, producers of steel forgings and steel castings in the rough or finished state up to sixty tons weight for marine, railway, mining, electrical and general engineering and for motor vehicle construction. Employees 2,000. These men are sharpening knives.

SAW GRINDING, SHEFFIELD. 1860.

SCYTHE GRINDING, SHEFFIELD. 1860.

Images are wood engravings published in *The Illustrated London News*, 6th Jan 1866 courtesy of The Wellcome Collection under 4.0 International (CC BY 4.0).

Sheffield had its problems for the firm, largely caused by the high price of fuel and American tariffs making it difficult for the company to compete pricewise in the US market; so the Jessops established a successful melting facility near New York. Many British steel-makers were of the view that the "Made in England" or "Made in Sheffield" marks were a major unique selling point for their produce, but Jessop differed and considered that they could use their Sheffield name on steel which was made in America.

Geoge Ibberson & Co, cutlery makers, probably the most famous and popular name in the Sheffield cutlery industry. From the mid-17th century to the beginning of the 19th century, there were just less than 100 Sheffield cutlers named Ibberson or Ibbotson. A cutler named William Ibberson operated in the Stannington area to the north west of Sheffield as long ago as 1666, but the origins of the George Ibberson company can be traced back to a Joseph Ibberson who made cutlery in 1700 in Norfolk Street. Ibberson became famous for producing the finest pocket knives featuring exotic handle materials like ivory, pearl and tortoiseshell. They also produced a wide range of cutlery, razors, scissors and sports knives. In 1873 the company registered its world famous Stradivarius Violin trademark with The Company of Cutlers in Hallamshire. This mark, along with Ibberson's other great trademark, Doublesharp ##, would gain legendary status amongst knife enthusiasts the world over.

Four cutlers working at benches with hammers and vices. The man in the centre is finishing off a knife. Coloured aquatint by R. Havell after G. Walker. Courtesy of The Wellcome Collection under 4.0 International (CC BY 4.0). *Life in England in aquatint and lithography, 1770-1860*: from the library of J. R. Abbey, San Francisco: Alan Wofsy Fine Arts, 1991, pp. 360-361, no. 432.40.

John Brown (1816 – 1896) was known as the Father of the South Yorkshire Iron Trade. He was born in Flavell's Yard, Fargate, the second son of Samuel Brown, a slater. John was educated at a local school held in a garret, and was apprenticed at age fourteen to Earl, Horton, & Co., factors, of Orchard Place, In 1831 they started making files and cutlery in Rockingham Street at the Hallamshire Works. In 1844 he set up John Brown & Company; manufacturing steel at a small foundry on the site which is now Orchard Square Shopping Centre and later moving to larger premises on Furnival Street.

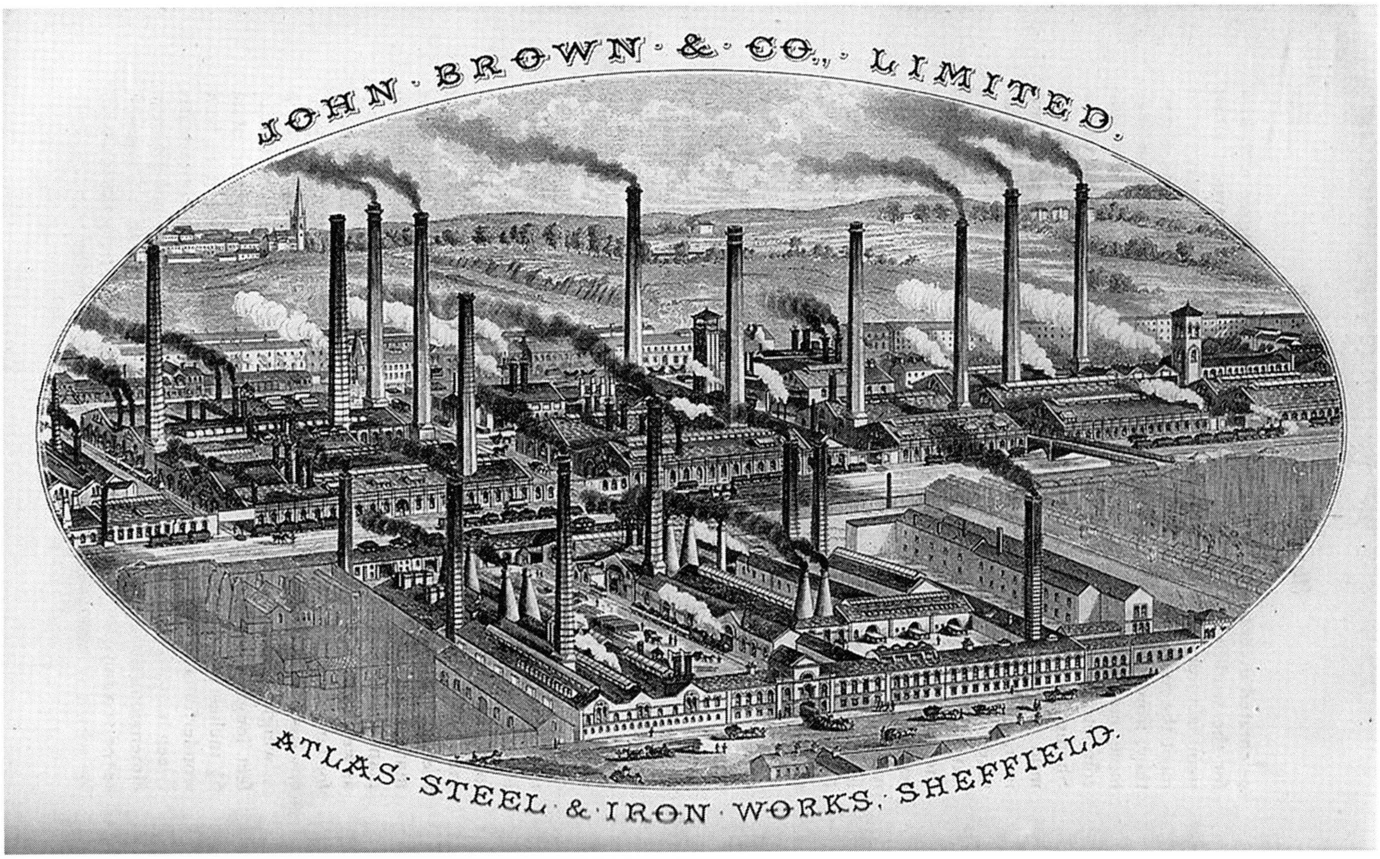

1879 engraving of Atlas Steel and Ironworks. All Saints Church (demolished 1977), which John Brown paid for in 1866-1869, can be seen in the background.

On New Year's Day 1856, Brown opened the Atlas Works in Brightside to consolidate his workshops and 4,000 strong workforce on a 3-acre site which within three years expanded to 30 acres. His greatest achievement was the development of armour plating for warships which came about when, at Toulon in 1860, he saw the French vessel *La Gloire* a timber-built 90-gun three-decker, cut down and coated with hammered plate armour, four and a half inches thick. This unnerved the English government so much that they ordered ten 90- and 100-gun vessels to be similarly adapted. Brown had concluded that the armoured plates might have been rolled and not hammered after visits by prime minister, Lord Palmerston, in April 1863 and from the lords of the admiralty during which they saw a plate rolled to twelve inches thick and fifteen to twenty feet long. The royal commission on armour plates ordered nearly all the plates they needed from Brown and in a few years, he had sheathed 75% of the British navy.

As well as armoured plate the Atlas Works was now manufacturing ordnance forgings, railway bars, steel springs, buffers, tyres, and axles, and was the first successfully to develop the Bessemer process, and to introduce into Sheffield the manufacture of steel rails.

This was the first technique for bulk steel production. This image shows a Bessemer Converter and is now outside Sheffield Industrial Museum at Kelham Island.

In 1902, Sheffield steelmakers John Brown & Company formed an association with Thomas Firth & Sons, the companies continuing under their own management until they finally merged in 1930 forming Firth Brown Ltd.

Shop floor conditions at Davy and United Engineering Company, Park Iron Works, 1957. Courtesy of The Wellcome Collection under 4.0 International (CC BY 4.0).

The Davy Brothers company was founded in 1830. In 1937 its name changed to Davy and United Engineering Co reflecting the agreement with United Engineering and Foundry Co of Pittsburgh that both companies would manufacture and sell the products of the other in their respective territories. Principal activities until the 1960s were manufacture of rolling mills and rolls for use in mills.

Kelham Island Industrial Museum

Kelham Island is one of the oldest industrial sites in Sheffield formed in the 1180s when a goit or millrace was created to carry water from the River Don to the Town Corn Mill, near Lady's Bridge. Things took off here in 1637 when the town armourer, Kellam Homer set up a grinding workshop and waterwheel on the island. The 1800s saw other industries emerge on the island not least in 1829 when John Crowley built a small iron foundry named Kelham Iron Works where he made boneshaker bicycles, corn grinders, lawn mowers as well as decorative items before moving his successful business to larger premises at Meadow Hall in 1870. In the 1890s the site was bought by the City. The Iron Works buildings were demolished and an electricity generating station was built in their place, to provide power for the City's new tram system.

The museum which opened in 1982 houses exhibitions on Sheffield science and industry, including examples of reconstructed little mesters' workshops and England's largest surviving Bessemer converter. A little mester is a self-employed worker who rents space in a factory or works from their own workshop; they worked alone or employed a small number of workers and/or apprentices and were involved in making cutlery and similar items such as woodworking chisels. The term applies almost exclusively to the craftsmen of the Sheffield area. Before the 18th century cutlery manufacture in Sheffield was by individual master craftsmen who would make an item from start to finish. In the late 18th century there was a growth in the complexity of the cutlery and tool industries that made it necessary for craftsmen to focus on a single stage of the manufacture. Cutlery factories then rented workshops to self-employed craftsmen, the little mesters, each specializing in one step of production, such as forging, grinding or finishing.

Alfred Beckett & Sons Ltd at the Brooklyn Works at Kelham viewed from Ball Bridge. The Brooklyn Works is a former site of steel, saw and file manufacture on Green Lane in the Kelham Island Quarter. The works are next to the listed industrial buildings of the Green Lane Works and Cornish Place in what has been called, "the most coherent stretch of industrial landscape in inner Sheffield". In 1967 Alfred Beckett & Sons was purchased by the Tempered Spring Company Ltd of Sheffield. (This is a photo of listed building number 1255043. By Enchufla Con Clave; This file is licensed under the Creative Commons Attribution-Share Alike 4.0 International licence.)

The Cementation Furnace

Close to Kelham Island is the cementation furnace – a Grade II Listed Building and the only surviving and intact example of this type of steel making furnace to survive in Britain. It is on Doncaster Street in the St Vincent's Quarter.

The furnace was built by Daniel Doncasters and Sons in 1848 to produce steel by the cementation process. By 1860 there were 250 cementation furnaces in Sheffield capable of producing 80,000 tons of blister steel; the striking large conical structures are characteristic of the city's industrial landscape. This furnace is the only remaining example which is undamaged although there are two others which are partially intact – at Bower Spring and Millsands. The Doncaster Street furnace operated throughout the Second World War with a blackout cover fitted to the furnace outlet which is still in place today, painted white. The furnace ceased operation in 1951.

The cementation process is an obsolete technology for making steel by carburization of iron (heating the iron in the presence of carbon such as charcoal so that it absorbs the carbon). Unlike modern steelmaking, it increased the amount of carbon in the iron. Derwentcote Steel Furnace near Newcastle-upon-Tyne built in 1720, is the earliest surviving example of a cementation furnace. The process begins with wrought iron and charcoal using one or more long stone pots inside a furnace. Typically, in Sheffield, each was 14 feet by 4 feet and 3.5 feet deep. Iron bars and charcoal are packed in alternating layers, with a top layer of charcoal and then refractory matter to make the pot or "coffin" airtight. Some manufacturers used a mixture of powdered charcoal, soot and mineral salts, called cement powder. In larger works, up to 16 tons of iron was treated in each cycle.

Fig. 16.—Cementation Furnaces—Messrs. Thomas Firth & Sons, Norfolk Works, Sheffield.

Cementation furnace at Thomas Frith & Sons' Norfolk Works.
From a Thomas Firth & Son promotional leaflet *c.* 1900.

Shepherd Wheel

Shepherd Wheel is a unique working example of Sheffield knife grinding industry. It was just one of many small water-powered grinding workshops along Sheffield's rivers and is the earliest complete example of this industry with evidence dating it back to the 1500s. By 1794 there were over 115 workshops of various kinds in existence along the rivers; today, Shepherd Wheel is almost all that remains of these small-scale sites.

The wheel itself is 5.5 metres high and 2 metres wide, and is made of cast and wrought iron, elm, oak and bronze. The water to turn the wheel comes from the large dam where water is diverted from the River Porter. The waterwheel turned twenty grindstones and several "glazing" stones, and powered two grinding workshops.

Abbeydale Industrial Hamlet

Abbeydale Industrial Hamlet is an industrial museum in the south of Sheffield which forms part of a former steel-working site on the River Sheaf, with a history going back to at least the 13th century. It consists of a number of dwellings and workshops that were formerly the Abbeydale Works – a scythe-making plant that was in operation until the 1930s – and is a remarkably complete example of a 19th-century works. The works are atypical in that much of the production process was completed on the same site in a manner similar to a modern factory. A more typical example of water-powered works in the area can be found at Shepherd Wheel.

The Council for the Conservation of Sheffield Antiquities explored and initiated the restoration of Abbeydale Works in 1964 and discovered the remains of six buildings in addition to those still standing. These were identified from a 1924 map of the site as a disused hardening shop; a disused open furnace shed; a lime and coke shed; a boiler house and chimney; the housing for the steam engine; a store for clay and anvils.

The works are Grade I listed and the workers' cottages, counting house, and manager's house are Grade II* listed. Abbeydale Industrial Hamlet is run as a working museum, with works and buildings dating from between 1714 and 1876. The museum demonstrates the process making blister steel from iron and coke, then refining this steel using techniques that originated with Benjamin Huntsman's invention of the crucible steel process. The river provides water power via a water wheel. There are several wheels on the site for driving a tilt hammer, for the initial forging of the scythe blades; grinding machinery, which also has steam installed as backup for times of drought, and a set of bellows. The blades were also hand forged for finishing.

Right: Abbeydale Industrial Hamlet: the crucible furnace building. (This file is licensed under the Creative Commons Attribution-Share Alike 2.0 Generic license. Attribution: Ashley Dace.)

A preserved drop forging hammer in Brightside. This can be seen near the site of the John Brown works it used to be part of. Forging is a manufacturing process involving the shaping of metal using localized compressive forces. The blows are delivered with a hammer (often a power hammer) or a die. Drop forging is a forging process where a hammer is raised and then "dropped" onto the workpiece to deform it according to the shape of the die. – Travail personnel (BulldozerD11). Creative Commons Attribution – Partage dans les Mêmes Conditions 3.0 (non transposée).

Don Cutlery Works. (Warofdreams licensed under the Creative Commons Attribution-Share Alike 3.0 Unported licence.)

The former Don Cutlery Works, on Doncaster Street in the Netherthorpe area; it was built in the 1850s for Southern & Richardson Ltd. The complex was occupied from *c.* 1860 until at least 1910 by Southern and Richardson, merchants and manufacturers of cutlery. A trade directory of *c.* 1880 lists them as manufacturers of silver plated tableware and pocket knives, razors and scissors. The buildings are now listed. Despite its obvious dereliction it survivives virtually intact and unaltered. Doncaster's Cementation Furnace is on the opposite side of the road. Other listed file and cutlery manufactures which have survived include the Kutrite Works in Snow Lane and Kingston Works in Walkley.

Confectionery

Yorkshire has been home to more confectionery companies over the years than any other region of Britain – and it's by no means just Rowntree's, Terry's and Mackintosh; there is a lot more to big Yorkshire chocolate than just York or Halifax. Needler's of Hull, Thornton's and Bassett's of Sheffield and Thorne's of Leeds have all been significant forces in the industry – the two Sheffield companies still are.

Bassett's: Founded in 1842 by George Bassett, Sheffield, 'wholesale confectioner, lozenge maker and British wine dealer', Bassett's opened its first factory in Portland Street in 1852 before moving to larger premises in Owlerton around 1900. Bassett's partner was Samuel Meggitt Johnson (his future son-in-law); they employed around 200 workers in what was the world's biggest sweet manufactory at the time. The Sheffield factory is today Cadbury's centre for sugar confectionery in the UK. Bassett's three most important brands are: liquorice allsorts, jelly babies, and wine gums.

Unclaimed Babies: Geo. Bassett & Co Ltd bought Wilkinsons of Pontefract, famous for their Pontefract cakes, Barratt's in 1966 (sherbet fountains and sweet cigarettes) and Trebor (the eponymous mints) before being bought themselves by Cadbury's in 1989. Jelly babies were originally conceived by an Austrian confectioner working for Fryers of Lancashire in the 1860s and branded as Unclaimed Babies. Bassett's jelly babies were launched in 1918 to celebrate the end of the First World War and were called Peace Babies. Production was halted during the Second World War, resuming in 1953 when rationing finally ended; they then became known as Jelly Babies. The Beatles were often pelted with them and successive Dr Whos have used them as a negotiating tool to take the steam out of tense situations. Screaming jelly babies are the dramatic result of a school experiment when the sweets are immersed in a strong oxidising agent.

Bertie Bassett: The origin of liquorice allsorts is legendary. In 1899, Charlie Thompson, a sales representative, was on a call in Leicester when he dropped a tray of samples all over the floor. These had already been rejected as individual purchases but the resulting colourful, random mix so impressed the shopkeeper that he placed an order for what was soon to become the Allsorts. Bertie Bassett is the Bassett company mascot, a man made entirely from liquorice allsorts created by John (Jack) McEwan and introduced to the sweet-buying public on 1st January 1929. He was obviously inspired by the highly successful Michelin Man. Today, the allsorts mix contains a son of Bertie: a diminutive aniseed and liquorice figure in Bertie's image

Betty Bassett: The *Doctor Who* serial 'The Happiness Patrol' featured the evil Kandy Man, who bore an uncanny likeness to Bertie Bassett. Bertie, however, triumphed: an out-of-court settlement led to oblivion for Kandy Man, sentenced to eternal exile. To celebrate his eightieth birthday in 2009, Bertie married his 'sweetheart' Betty Bassett (no relation we hope) in the Sheffield factory with workers enjoying the ceremony as guests including even a best man.

Liquorice-Free Allsorts: By 1966 Bassett's were the largest sugar confectionery manufacturers in Britain employing 1,300 people. They now also produce varieties of allsorts devoid of liquorice: fruit allsorts feature mixed-fruit flavours; dessert allsorts include apple tart and lemon cheesecake. There is also a red liquorice Betty Bassett.

Thornton's – a toffee tin. Joseph William Thornton left his job as a sales representative for the Don Confectionery Company in 1911 and opened his first Thornton's Chocolate Kabin shop on the corner of Norfolk Street and Howard Street. Products included Violet Cachous, Sweet-Lips, Phul-Nanas and Curiously Strong Mints. Chocolate production began in 1913 in the back room of their second shop on the Moor. Easter eggs and Thorntons Special Toffee were the main lines until the 1950s when the Continental Chocolates range was launched. In 1948 the company moved to Belper and in 1954, Walter Willen, a Swiss confectioner, joined and created Swiss Assortment – a range of handmade confectionery. The name had to be changed to Continental Assortment after complaints from the Swiss Embassy.

Don Confectionery Co, Sheffield: Somewhat unfairly, the Don Confectionery Co is best remembered as the company which Joseph Thornton left in 1911 to set up on his own. Don Confectionery was established by Samuel Meggitt Johnson in 1878; Johnson was managing director of Bassett's but he needed somewhere for George Bassett's two sons to work, apparently, because he did not want them in the Bassett's business. However, the company was bought by Bassett's in 1933.

A. L. Simpkin & Co Ltd, Sheffield: This company was founded in 1921 by Albert Leslie Simpkin. They were the first manufacturers of travel sweets. High quality glucose confections using natural flavours and colours were sold in chemists' shops, a niche market which avoided competition with the large confectionery manufacturers. By 1924 Simpkin had 80 per cent coverage of the UK with 12,000 accounts, and employed 180 workers. The range was extended from bulk barley sugar drops in jars to include powdered sweets in 8 oz reasonably airtight travel tins containing barley sugar drops which can alleviate the symptoms of travel sickness. Today, domestic sales are still mainly through chemist and health food outlets.

Other Industry

Henderson's Relish: The sign on the now closed factory faces on to Leavygrave Road. Henry Henderson began manufacturing sauce in the latter part of the 19th century at 35 Broad Lane. Henderson's Relish is still being made. The company was bought by Shaws of Huddersfield in 1910 who still supply Hendersons with vinegar. The Henderson's factory was located opposite what was once Jessop's Hospital for Women, now the Music Department of the University of Sheffield. (Chemical Engineer. Attribution 4.0 International (CC BY 4.0)).

Vickers was established as a steel foundry by the miller Edward Vickers and his father-in-law George Naylor in 1828. Naylor was a partner in the foundry Naylor & Sanderson; Vickers' brother William owned a steel rolling operation. Vickers began by making steel castings and quickly became famous for casting church bells. In 1854 Vickers' sons Thomas and Albert joined the business – Tom Vickers as a metallurgist and Albert as a team-builder and salesman – and were key to its subsequent rapid development. In 1863 the company moved to a new site in Sheffield on the River Don in Brightside.

The company went public in 1867 as Vickers, Sons & Company and gradually diversified into marine shafts and marine propellers. In 1882 they set up a forging press. Vickers produced their first armour plate in 1888 and their first artillery piece in 1890. They bought out the Barrow Shipbuilding Company in 1897, acquiring its subsidiary the Maxim Nordenfelt Guns and Ammunition Company to become Vickers, Sons & Maxim. In 1911 Vickers Ltd expanded into aircraft manufacture and a Vickers School of Flying was opened at Brooklands in 1912. The famously dependable Vickers machine gun was in service from before the First World War until the 1960s.

Vickers celebrating the end of the First World War.

Interior of Gun and Crank Finishing Shop, showing machines boring, turning, and rifling guns, 1897. Originally published in *Grace's Guide*.

Mining

No.1199. Coal Strike.1912.Poor digging for coal. Sheffield.

Because of the preponderance of the steel industry in Sheffield we tend to forget that the city and its surrounding area supported a large and economically important mining industry. Coal has been mined in the area since the 13th century; in 1869 there were some 35 working collieries in the Sheffield area. By 1929 a map published by the *Sheffield Telegraph* showed 73 collieries. Limestone quarrying has been important too: the Palace of Westminster in London was built using limestone from quarries in the nearby village of Anston.

Striking miners work a seam of coal they have discovered on a building site off Handsworth Road in Darnall, Sheffield during the 1893 dispute. Scanned from *The History of the City of Sheffield 1843-1993*.

Drift mine from around 1900 near Newman Road.

From 1868 Nunnery Colliery was operated by the Waverley Coal Company who also worked High Hazels Colliery about three miles to the east. It is reputed that coal mined from Nunnery supplied half the houses in Sheffield as well as local businesses. On 3rd December 1923 an accident caused by the breaking of a rope hauling an underground Paddy Mail train, carrying 90 men and 30 boys, killed seven people while around 50 others were injured. The inquest jury returned a verdict of "accidental death." Paddy mails were operated by railway contractors, on temporary tracks laid to remove spoil from their workings, and to transport workers from their shanty villages to the work site. Many of these navvies were of Irish origin, hence the name given to the trains.

Photograph originally published in J.P. Turley *Sheffield's Yesterdays – Places, People and Pubs* (1993)

Blade inspection at Swann-Morton, 1950s. Courtesy and © Swann-Morton Ltd.

In August 1932 WR Swann, JA Morton and Doris Fairweather founded the business to manufacture and sell razor blades. After years of research and development the emphasis was changed from razor blades to surgical blades. By 1957 Swann-Morton was producing over 38 million blades each year. Mindful of the future security of the company, the workforce and its founding principles, a trust was formed to administer the company within which the employees had a 50% share and the remaining 50% placed in a charitable trust. Swann-Morton remain leaders in the field today from their premises in Owlerton Green.

Blackburn Meadows cooling towers 2003. Author Chris Bell, Creative Commons Attribution Share-alike license 2.0.

Tinsley Towers demolition 24 August 2008: Going, going, going…

> I always felt I was back up north when driving over the Tinsley Viaduct on the M1 with the cooling towers on my right. They were a powerful symbol of Sheffield's industrial heritage and are a great loss. Tinsley Viaduct is the first two-tier road bridge in the United Kingdom. The cooling towers were left standing for safety reasons for 30 years after the demolition of the Blackburn Meadows Power Station which they served.

Author johnthescone from Sheffield. This file is licensed under the Creative Commons Attribution 2.0 Generic license.

Children's Entertainment

Denby Street Nursery School, 1949.

Children outside the Stocksbridge Palace, Manchester Road. Smiling faces at the Matinee Club with *William Comes to Town* on the bill – a 1948 British comedy based on the 'Just William' series of novels by Richmal Crompton. Jon Pertwee was in it. The story line goes: William Brown and his gang the Outlaws visit the Prime Minister in Downing Street to demand shorter school hours and better pay for kids. The newspaper publicity caused by their visit lands William and his friends in trouble with their parents. William almost ruins his chances of going to the circus (his parents made him promise to stay out of trouble), but somehow he finally gets there. The Palace opened in 1921 with seating for 1,000. The first film was *Kismet*; the first talkie was *Let Us Be Gay* screened in 1931. Bernard Dore, Uncle Bernard, was manager for 18 years; he set up the Matinee Club and performed conjuring tricks, organised outings and introduced the basics of road safety to the children. The Palace closed in 1966.

Thornseat Lodge, home for toddlers, Mortimer Rd, Bradfield Dale 1952 was originally built as a shooting lodge for William Jessop, the steel magnate. It became a children's home in the 30's until the early 80's. This post from Sheffieldforum.co.uk captures the place: 'It was still a childrens' home in the 70's. I worked there. I took a job as it was going to be an intermediate treatment centre where kids from the city could spend short times away from the pressures of their environment. Unfortunately it became a long stay home and I did not feel it right that kids from the city were living in a false environment long term when they would have to return to their natural home one day. In those days the place was impressive. The office was called the cedar room because it was just that, floor, walls and ceiling, all cedar and when you entered it you could smell it. There were intricate carvings all round and in each corner was a carving of the head of William Jessop. The lounge had a big open fireplace at one end and that was also hand carved with hunting scenes. Unfortunately, someone had stripped the varnish from it and the wood had dried out and was starting to crack. I had a room which looked straight down the valley to Sheffield, wonderful. Never used them but there were snow shoes in the cellar in case of being snowed in. The maintenance man was a wonderful local man with a wonderful name "Mr Merryweather".

Flooding

Storm damage in Clyde Road, Heeley, 1958 – with attitude.

Ceg-fepsys publishes chronologies of historical flash flood events from newspaper archives and other sources, dating from the 1700s. Here is the entry for July 2nd 1958: 'One of the most badly affected areas was Sheffield where flooding was reported as the worst since the city's great flood in 1864 when the Dale Dyke reservoir burst its banks. Rain commenced during the early afternoon of the 1st and continued until noon the next day with only a break of little over an hour during the morning of the 2nd. Rain was heavy at times  and some of the heaviest rain occurred over the Totley and Burbage Moors where, around midnight on the 1st-2nd more than 1 inch fell in less than 30 minutes. Fed by this heavy rain the River Sheaf burst its banks in a number of places, and there was flooding in the Millhouses, Abbeydale, Heeley and Low-field areas. Further into the city where the Sheaf joins the Don, thousands of houses were flooded, bridges destroyed and the Midland Railway Station put out of action for several hours by flood-water and debris'.

Flooding can be fun – Surbiton Street 1954.

Sheffield Characters and Culture

Sheffield Cleaning Department. One of those Forth Bridge jobs by the looks of it…

Amy Johnson was born in 1903 in Hull and was educated at Boulevard Municipal Secondary School (later Kingston High School) and the University of Sheffield where she graduated with a degree in economics. Today the "Amy Johnson Building" houses the department of Automatic Control and Systems Engineering at the University. Johnson gained worldwide fame when, in 1930, she became the first woman to fly solo from England to Australia. Flying G-AAAH Jason, she left Croydon Airport on 5th May and landed at Darwin, Northern Territory on 24th May 11,000 miles later.

In the Grass, Arthur Hughes (1832–1915) 1864. Museums Sheffield's oil collection comprises over 1,950 paintings and spans the city's visual art, social history and Ruskin collections. The Modern British collection is one of the most important in the country outside of the Tate. It includes works by many of Britain's most significant 20th century artists including Gwen John, Stanley Spencer, Vanessa Bell, David Bomberg, Frank Auerbach and Bridget Riley. Paintings by artists such as Paul Cézanne and Alfred Sisley are included in the European 20th century collection. Artists represented in the 16th to 19th century collections include John Singer Sargent, Thomas Gainsborough, J. M. W. Turner, Peter Lely and the Pre-Raphaelite artists Edward Burne-Jones, Dante Gabriel Rossetti and John Everett Millais.

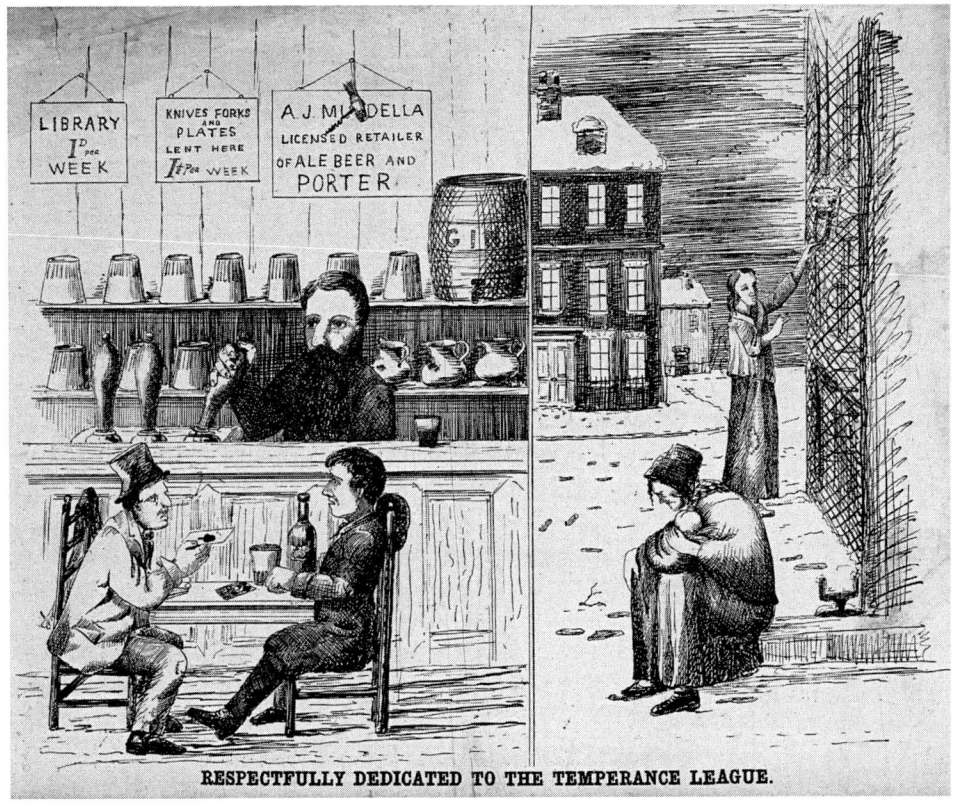

Sheffield played a prominent role in the Temperance Movement. The British Temperance League's offices, originally in Preston, moved to Sheffield in 1880, first to Furnival Street and then to Union Street and later still in 1940 to Livesey-Clegg House also in Union Street. Sheffield's temperance hall in Townhead Street was destroyed by enemy bombs during the Second World War.

Above: Dore and Totley Station, July 1960. The photo shows pupils from Ripley Secondary Technical School (now merged with Mill Hill School), changing trains to go on to Edale for a biology field trip. The station was opened by the Midland Railway, for passengers only, as Dore and Totley in 1872 on the then two-year-old Midland Main Line extension from Chesterfield to Sheffield.

Left: John Robert "Joe" Cocker OBE (20th May 1944 – 22nd December 2014) Cocker in 1969, as pictured on the cover of his second album, Joe Cocker! He was born at 38 Tasker Road, Crookes, the youngest son of a civil servant, Harold Cocker, and Madge Cocker, née Lee. Depending on who you believe he got his nickname, Joe, either from playing a childhood game called "Cowboy Joe", or from a local window cleaner named Joe. He is not related to fellow Sheffield-born musician Jarvis Cocker, although Joe was a friend of the family and even babysat Jarvis as a boy. In 1961 Cocker formed a new group, Vance Arnold and the Avengers playing in the pubs of Sheffield, performing covers of Chuck Berry and Ray Charles songs. He then developed an interest in blues music; in 1963, the group booked their first significant gig when they supported the Rolling Stones at Sheffield City Hall.

Margaret Drabble (b. 1939)

"When I go back to Sheffield I feel very close to it – although the whole family has moved away, there's something about the people, about the manners that I recognise."

– Margaret Drabble

Born in Nether Edge, Sheffield, the second daughter of lawyer and novelist John F. Drabble and the teacher and Newnham, Cambridge, graduate Kathleen Marie (née Bloor). She is a younger sister of the novelist and critic A.S. Byatt. After evacuation to Pontefract, wartime bombing forced a prudent family relocation to strategically less important York. Drabble, like her sister, was educated at the prestigious Quaker Mount School at York, where her mother was on the teaching staff; Judi Dench was a contemporary: Margaret (fairy Moth), sister Susan (Hippolyta) and Judi Dench (Titania) all performed together in *A Midsummer's Night Dream*. Drabble then won a major scholarship to Newnham College, Cambridge, where she read English and gained a starred First. She joined the Royal Shakespeare Company at Stratford in 1960, but left to write.

Len Doherty (1930-1983) has been described as being "among the most important practitioners of the socialist novel in Britain." by Philip Bounds in *Orwell and Marxism: The Political and Cultural Thinking of George Orwell*, London: I B Tauris, 2009. He was born in working class Maryhill, Glasgow and moved with his family to Yorkshire in the 1940s taking work as a miner at the age of seventeen. While working at Thurcroft Colliery near Rotherham he joined the local Communist Party and was one of a number of working class writers of the period sponsored by the Party and published by Communist Party company Lawrence & Wishart. His first novel, *A Miner's Sons*, (1955) is acknowledged as one of the most successful socialist and social novels. 1957 saw publication of Doherty's second novel *The Man Beneath*; about the same time he left the Communist Party and joined the staff of the *Sheffield Star*. His third novel, *The Good Lion*, was published in 1958 to critical acclaim; it is a book which owes much to Doherty's own experiences in the industrial landscapes around Sheffield.

Fred Priest is the author's great, great uncle. Here he is standing second on the right in this team photo of the 1901 FA Cup Final team. Alfred Ernest Priest (24th July 1875 – 5th May 1922) was born in South Bank, Middlesbrough and played for Darlington and South Bank before joining Sheffield United in 1896; they allegedly signed him while he was sat in a bath in Newcastle, after South Bank had played there. On 17th March 1900 he helped England beat Ireland 2-0 in a British Championship match at Lansdowne Road, Ballsbridge, Dublin.

He made his debut for The Blades in the Football League First Division in the 1896-97 season, playing mainly as outside left, and helped United win the Football League championship in 1897-98. He also won the 1899 and 1902 FA Cup finals with Sheffield United. He was living at 8 Guest Road in Ecclesall.

By 1911 Alfred Ernest was a professional football club manager living at 4 Sandringham Road in West Hartlepool and married to Ann, but their first son died before he reached his first birthday. They had eight children in total including Ronald, Florence, Eric (my great uncle) and Olive.

After 209 league appearances and 72 goals, Fred returned to his native Teesside when South Bank FC re-signed him in December 1905. Middlesbrough FC signed him in October 1906 as a player and assistant trainer; he made thirteen league appearances. Two years later, in the summer of 1909, he crossed the River Tees to join the newly formed Hartlepools United FC as their player-manager. He retired from playing in December 1908 after which he became a licensee at the Market Hotel, Lynn Street, West Hartlepool but died of cirrhosis of the liver aged 46 and is buried in an unmarked grave in West View Cemetery, West Hartlepool.

On 11th October 1922, Hartlepools United FC played Sheffield United FC (a team including several Wednesday FC players). The gate money was given to his widow and young family.

Sheffield United were formed in 1889, as a spin-off of Sheffield United Cricket Club; playing football in the winter months was seen as a good way for the cricketers to keep fit.

Sheffield United won the First Division in 1898 and the FA Cup in 1899, 1902, 1915 and 1925; they were First Division runners-up in 1897 and 1900 and reached the FA Cup final in 1901 and 1936. United were the first club in English football to achieve promotion from the newly formed Second Division to the First Division in 1892–93. The club was also a founder member of the Premier League in the 1992–93 season, during which they scored the first ever goal of the competition; Brian Deane was the first scorer in a 2–1 win at Bramall Lane against Manchester United. Sheffield United are one of only five sides to have won all four professional divisions of English football.

Ebenezer Elliott (1781–1849), whose statue is in Weston Park, was known as the 'Corn Law Rhymer' for leading the fight to repeal the Corn Laws which were causing extreme hardship and starvation among the poor. Though an iron factory owner himself, his devotion to the welfare of the labouring classes won him a sympathetic international reputation long after his poetry ceased to be read. Elliott went into the steel business in Sheffield with a capital of one hundred pounds, and after many health-related and financial struggles had amassed a handsome fortune by 1829. He was born at the New Foundry, Masbrough, in the parish of Rotherham but much of his activism took place in and around Sheffield. Fighting for the repeal of the Corn Laws became the defining issue in his life. He formed the first society in England to call for reform of the Corn Laws: the Sheffield Mechanics' Anti-Bread Tax Society founded in 1830. In 1834 he was instrumental in the establishment of the Sheffield Anti-Corn Law Society and the Sheffield Mechanics' Institute. He was active in the Sheffield Political Union and campaigned vigorously for the 1832 Reform Act. He was later active in Chartist agitation, acting as the Sheffield delegate to the Great Public Meeting in Westminster in 1838, and chairing the meeting in Sheffield where the Charter was introduced to local people.

Elliott's "cloud-rolling Sheffield". One of the illustrations from the above article beginning "One beauty of Sheffield is that you can see very little of it at a time." *Harper's Magazine* 8, 1884.

Three Soldiers Being Served in a Café (1939-1945) by Charles Alfred Mozley (1914 –1991), artist, teacher, prolific book illustrator and designer of book covers, posters and prints. He was born in Darnall, Sheffield, and, while still a schoolboy, attended the Sheffield School of Art. An exhibition of his artworks was held at the Hibbert Brothers Gallery in the city in 1933. After a year spent teaching in Sheffield, Mozley won a scholarship to the Royal College of Art, in 1934.

Charles Mozley: *War Weapons Event in a Town Centre* (1939 – 1945)

These images were created and released by the Imperial War Museum. Photographs taken, or artworks created, by a member of the forces during their active service duties are covered by Crown Copyright provisions. Faithful reproductions may be reused under that licence, which is considered expired 50 years after their creation.

Three splendid photographs of Sheffield Fire Brigade. In 1869 the Sheffield Town Council took over the responsibility for fire cover from the Insurance Brigades. The decision was given weight by a number of large fires between 1865 and 1869: namely at the Surrey Theatre, West Bar; Mr. Burrell's, Draper, Snig Hill; The Ragged Schools and Mudfords Rope Works, Exchange Street. In 1869 the first fire station was in Norfolk Street opposite Milk Street. Mr. Pound, Superintendent of the Brigade, had to form the new brigade with fifteen young police constables and for eleven months living quarters were a problem as many of the men lived as far away as Spital Hill. When a fire occurred at night the men were called off their beats by whistle, and in the daytime Mr. Pound had to collect any constable he could find.

Milk-maid at Dobbin Hill Top Farm, Ecclesall in the 1890s.

Fullwood Road, Ranmoor, JF Eardley's chemist to left – still the Ranmoor Pharmacy today, WH Broughton's grocer shop to its right with post office next door.

Cinemas

The Empire Palace Theatre Of Varieties opened in November 1895 on Union Street with its frontage taking up most of Charles Street; in later years it was known simply as the Sheffield Empire and had seating for 2,500. By 1896 it was showing 'animated pictures' in its variety programmes using a 'Variety Lumiere Cinematographe'. The artists who appeared at the Empire Theatre is a veritable 'Who's Who' of music hall and variety stars, including Marie Lloyd, Florrie Ford, Harry Lauder, George Formby, Grace Fields, Anna Pavlova, Ivor Novello; Hylda Baker, Jimmy Clitheroe, Ken Dodd, Shirley Bassey, Tommy Steele, and Harry Secombe. It closed in 1959 and was demolished.

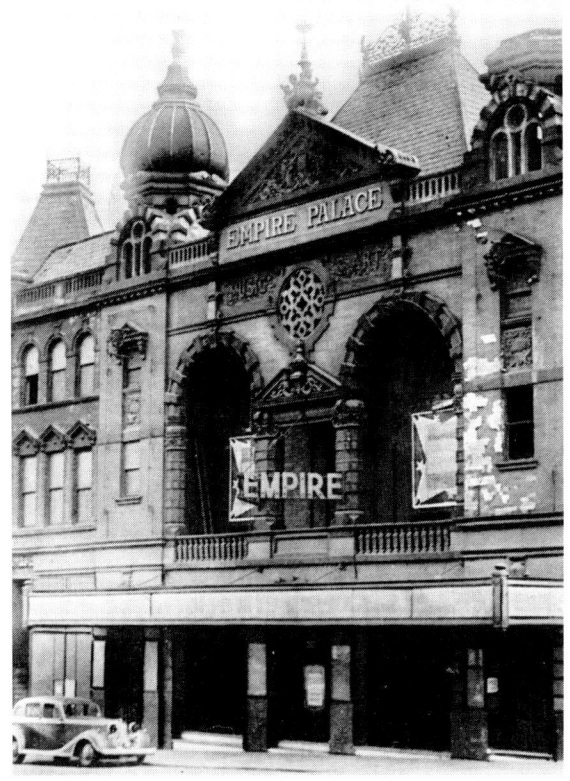

Cinema House, Fargate opened on 6th May 1913 with its marvellous glazed white faience tower above the cinema entrance. You entered into a Jacobean style hall; the auditorium seated 800 and continued the Jacobean theme. In 1959 the cinema owners sold the building. The final show on 12th August 1961 featured John Wayne in *The Horse Soldiers* and Burt Lancaster in *The Devil's Disciple*.

The Rex Cinema was built on Mansfield Road in the Intake district of Sheffield and opened on Monday 24th July 1939 with Fred MacMurray in *Men With Wings*. It came about on the instigation T.W. Ward, the Sheffield steel works owner, and was designed on simplistic modern lines. It was run as a family house where 'X' certificate films were seldom shown. Children's Saturday matinees were introduced in 1958; it never opened on Sundays until 1981. The Rex Cinema survived longer than all of Sheffield's other local cinemas and was one of the few not to turn to bingo. The building was demolished in October 1983.

Opened as the Electra Palace in 1911 in Fitzalan Square on the former 'Wonderland' site which was a wooden fairground where 'animated pictures' were one of the entertainments. The exterior was reminiscent of 15th century Arabian architecture in white glazed terracotta. The cinema closed for refurbishment in 1945 and re-opened on September 9th 1945 as the News Theatre. In 1959 it changed its name to The Cartoon Cinema with continuous showings of cartoons and news films. In 1962 it was bought by the Classic Cinemas chain (*right*). It changed hands again in 1982 when it was bought by the Canon Cinema group. After a serious fire in February 1984 the cinema was demolished and redeveloped for retail.

The Gaumont Cinema seen here in the 1950s. It opened on 26th December 1927 as the Regent with seating for 1,450 in the stalls and 850 in the balcony all in neo-Classical/Italian Renaissance style. In July 1946 it was re-named Gaumont Theatre and in the '60s played host to Cliff Richard, Eddie Cochran, Bobby Darin, The Rolling Stones and The Beatles. The Gaumont closed on 7th November 1985 with *Perfect*, Madonna in *Desperately Seeking Susan* and *A View to a Kill*.

Wicker Cinema. Studio 5, 6 & 7 in the Wicker Sheffield, near to the Wicker Railway Bridge, opened as the Wicker Picture House on 14th June 1920. The exterior was in white faience with Grecian urns running along a top parapet. With circle and stalls, the cinema sat 1,080. The roof of the cinema was damaged during the Sheffield blitz in 1940.

The Grade II listed Adelphi Picture Theatre is in the Attercliffe district in the east of Sheffield. It opened on 18th October 1920.

Pubs

Fagan's, Broad Lane, and 'The Snog'. Fagan's was originally called 'The Barrel'; it features on an 1815 map of the area showing that the current left-hand room was, at that time, a next door tenement, the pub and the tenement sharing a yard at the rear of the property. Fagan's has seen only three licensees in the past 104 years: Bomber Command veteran Joe Fagan ran the pub from 1947 to 1985 and was Tetley's longest serving landlord; Joe died only a few weeks after passing on the tenancy to the next landlord, Tom Boulding. On the front right of the pub is a tiny snug originally called the dram shop – a name for a pub room only found in the Sheffield area. The sign over the door says, in Japanese, "We install and service hangovers.". In the 19th century, the pub was owned by local brewer, Rawsons. In turn ownership passed to Gilmours, Tetleys, Allied Breweries and, currently, Punch Taverns. In April 2013 Sheffield artist Pete McKee, famous for his comic cartoon paintings, adorned the gable end of Fagan's with 'The Snog'. At the time, this was his largest mural.

The Old Queen's Head in Post Hill is the oldest domestic building in the city. This timber framed delight dates from c.1475; the earliest known written record of it is in an inventory compiled in 1582 of the estate of George Talbot, the 6th Earl of Shrewsbury that included the furnishings of the building, which was then called "The hawle at the Poandes". The 'hawle' probably refers to a banqueting hall for parties hunting wildfowl in the nearby ponds. These ponds, which formed in the area where the Porter Brook meets the River Sheaf, are long gone, but are remembered in the local names Pond Street, Pond Hill (formerly Pond Well Hill) and Ponds Forge. By the beginning of the 19th century the building was a residence. In 1840 a pub called the Old Queen's Head was opened in the neighbouring building, and sometime after 1862 the pub expanded into this building, Grade II* listed status since 1952. The Queen in the pub's name is Mary, Queen of Scots, who was imprisoned in Sheffield from 1570 to 1584.

The Ship Inn, Shalesmoor, Kelham Island. The Ship boasts a stunning tiled façade by Henry Tomlinson Ltd's brewery. On reopening after a 2015 refit general manager, Christy Beardshaw, said: "It's a wonderful thing that we've managed to preserve so much of the Ship Inn – it has been standing for almost 200 years and even survived the flood caused by the Dale Dyke dam burst in 1864". Henry Tomlinson Ltd's Anchor Brewery in Cherry Street was wrecked in 1940 in an air raid. They merged with Carter, Milner & Bird Ltd in 1942 to form Hope & Anchor Breweries Ltd which was used as a packing station for export beer to the troops in 1945.

The Roebuck Tavern, Charles Street. Remarkable as an oasis of history in a desert of modernity.

The five storey Bell Hagg Inn was on Manchester Road, near to the 416 metre long Bell Hagg Street. It was built in 1832 as a tea house and was also known as The John Thomas. It closed in 2005.

The Rutland Arms in Brown Street is a wonderfully quirky old building which still impresses today. Duncan Gilmour & Co Ltd was founded as a wine and spirits merchant in Queen St in 1831, moving to Dixon Street in 1860. In 1906 they bought Birks & Co of the Lady's Bridge Brewery at 9 Bridge Street (founded by Edward Nanson in 1791 and sold to William Henry Birks in 1858). Other acquisitions were Dearden's High House Brewery in 1901; Whitmarsh, Watson & Co in 1906 with 140 pubs; and William Greaves and Co Ltd in 1920. Duncan Gilmour & Co Ltd were themselves taken over by Tetley's in 1954 along with their 342 public houses.

Phlegm on the wall. "Surrounded by galleries, studios and creative offices…the Rutland and its hydrangea-abundant beer garden fill up quickly on Friday evenings, when nearby artists and workers down tools. In the spirit of this creative part of town, the pub's exterior is decorated with the distinctive work of street artist Phlegm while mini exhibitions by local artists often hang on the walls inside". – https://www.ourfaveplaces.co.uk/where-to-go/rutland-arms/

The Three Tuns is another wonderful building and is a Flatiron-style edifice between Silver Street Head and Lee Croft. *The Morning Advertiser* (8th August 2016) told how the building used to be a nun's washhouse on a road leading from the cathedral to a convent; there are apparently tunnels beneath the building connecting the cathedral with the nunnery.

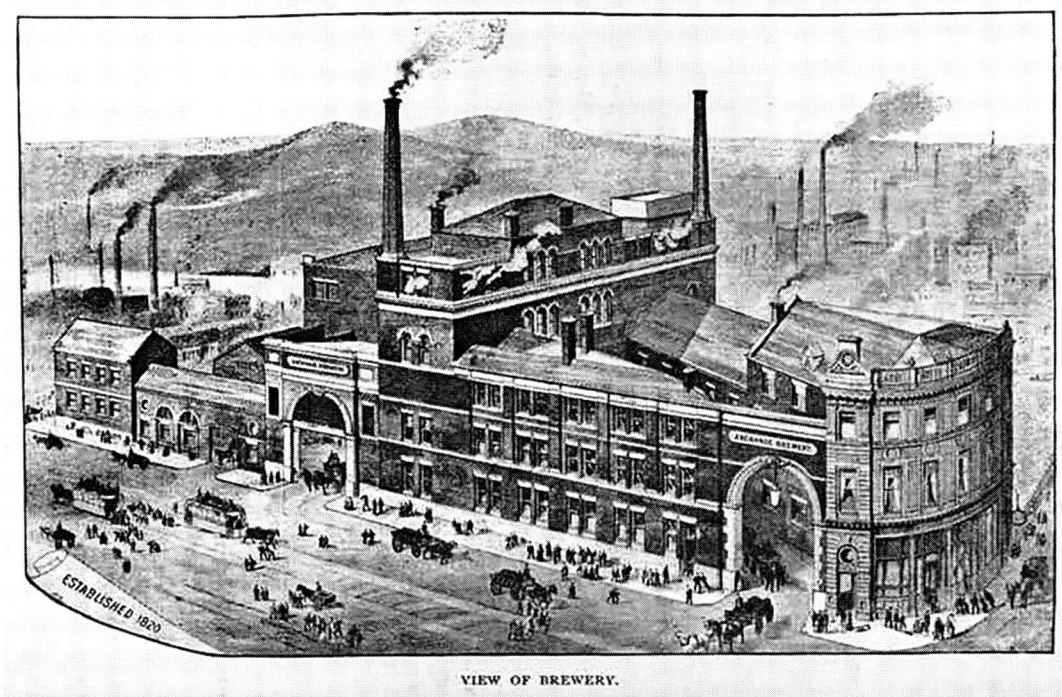

VIEW OF BREWERY.

Tennant Brothers Ltd was founded in 1820 by Proctor & Co in Market Place but acquired by Edward and Robert Tennant in 1840 moving to Bridge Street in 1852 where the Exchange Brewery was built. Whitbread took them over in 1962 along with their 700 licensed houses. The Exchange was run under the name Whitbread East Pennines.

Waiting for opening time at the Milton Arms at 272 Rockingham Street.

Sheffield Businesses

Right: L & A Wilkinson, booksellers and stationers at 26 Norfolk Market Hall about 1900. Books and stationery were all very well but the Wilkinsons clearly had an eye on the future when they expanded into phonographs and records – making this one of Sheffield's earliest record shops, also selling playing cards and postcards. The store was an agent for the world famous Edison phonographs. Love the hats. Whole sections of shops were given over to stocks of postcards. Most postcards were made from card – but others made of wood, copper, silk and coconut are known. The collecting of postcards became all the rage and is the world's fourth largest collecting hobby after stamps, coins and banknotes.

Above: A. Cooper – Confectioner and sponge sandwich specialist (Victoria sponge).

Right: Pease – Confectioner and grocer. Tea, chocolate and cigarettes on sale here: the stock in trade for Edwardian grocers. The three leading English chocolate makers are well represented; Rowntree, Cadbury and Fry all of which were established by Quakers.

In 1296 a royal charter to hold markets and fairs in Sheffield was granted by Edward I to Thomas de Furnival, Lord of the Manor of Sheffield. For the next 600 years or so markets were owned and operated by the lords of the manor. Towards the end of the 18th century the problems and nuisance caused by the increased number of animals being driven into the town centre for sale promoted local inhabitants to petition the owner of the markets, Charles Howard the Earl of Surrey (later the 11th Duke of Norfolk), to provide them with a larger market place with better access for animals, carts and pedestrians. In 1786 – a new market hall, Fitzalan Market, was built on site of the old market.

In 1847 the 14th Duke approved plans for a new fruit and vegetable market on the site of the Tontine Inn; which would become the Norfolk Market Hall when it opened in 1850. In 1899 Sheffield Corporation purchased the markets from the 15th Duke for £526,00 and since that time the markets have been the property of Sheffield City Council. The 20th century has brought gradual closure and consolidation of the markets, Fitzalan Market Hall closed in 1930, and the Norfolk Market Hall in 1959.

Castlefolds fruit & veg market in the 1930s at what looks to be setting up time with all the delivery carts and vehicles. Castlefolds Markets was established in 1847 on land between the Corn Exchange and the Norfolk Market Hall. The Sheaf Open Market was began on the adjacent site. Castlefolds closed on 4th November, 1961 when the Parkway Wholesale Market was opened.

In 1929 the Markets Department produced a handbook which described Sheaf Market: "*The Sheaf Market is rather unique in its character, being a very large open market, and is chiefly used on Tuesdays and Saturdays... Traders dealing in all classes of commodities attend, and the section used by the local fruit and vegetable growers, which is an early morning market, is let to Crockery sellers on the two market days. In the spring-time the market is crowded with plants and flowers.*"

Sheaf Market 1964. The handbook also stated that, "Formally [sic] the Live Poultry Market was held in the cellars under the Castlefolds Market, but this was found to be a very unsatisfactory situation, and it was transferred to a more suitable building in the Sheaf Market which had been used as a flour mill. Quite recently the interior has been fitted with up-to-date wire cages which entirely comply with requirement of the RSPCA. A very large business in live poultry is carried on here, also persons requiring defenders for their homes in the shape of canine friends are able to find their requirements in the market."

The Royal Cutlery Works, 99, Norfolk Street, 1919. Mappin & Webb has over 240 years of tradition and historical significance in the world of silver and fine jewellery. It's a story that began in 1775, when Jonathan Mappin opened a workshop in Fargate, Sheffield. His mission was to create the most beautifully crafted silverware for (affluent) British society. Girls as young as 6 were employed to grind forks. Women were allocated the most tedious, dirty and dangerous jobs such as feeding spoon blanks through the rollers at Mappin & Webb in 1920. In 1859 the four brothers in Mappin Bros.quarrelled and the youngest, John, left to set up Mappin & Co at The Royal Cutlery Works on Pond Hill. He recruited his brother in law George Webb to join his firm, and by 1868 they were known as Mappin & Webb & Co. It was in 1903 that Mappin & Webb bought Mappin Bros, and became Mappin & Webb (Mappin Bros incorporated) and the firms were finally united.In 1922 Mappin & Webb moved to a new factory on Queen's Road called the Royal Works, which they claimed was 'one of the largest and best equipped of its kind in the United Kingdom'. It covered 15,000 square yards and employed nearly 1000 people. In the 1930s their key markets were hotels, restaurants and steamships, and a single order for the hospitality industry could consist of up to 20,000 pieces of cutlery'.

February 15th 1913 saw the first motorbus begin operation between Broomhill and Lodge Moor supplementing Sheffield's existing tram network.

G.I. Crapper, Chaff Merchant in 1913. George Israel Crapper and his team sold hay, straw and chop –everything a horse could want. His premises were in Langsett Road. Chaff or chopped hay and/or straw is fed to horses and ponies to stop them bolting their feed. Chop was chopped animal feeds, mainly from rye.

The Sheffield Shelter for Lost and Starving Cats has been caring for stray and unwanted cats and kittens for over 120 years. It was founded in 1897 by Miss Jane Barker in Broomspring Lane before moving to Gell Lane, and then to Travis Place in 1964. Re-homing around 400 cats per year, they provide a safe refuge, medical treatment – whatever the cost.

Here comes the coke van – this delivery is in the village of Grindleford in Derbyshire in 1920. Under a 1917 Act of Parliament Sheffield United Gas Light Company, 1844-1917, became the Sheffield Gas Co., 1917-1938, and it set about acquiring gas works in the region to create a large supply network that became known as the Sheffield Grid. Consequently, Tinsley Park Colliery Co. (1918), Orgreave Colliery (1918), Rother Valley Colliery Co. (1919), United Stell Companies (1919), Nunnery Colliery Co. (1928), High Hazels Colliery and Thorncliffe Coal Distillation Co. were all purchased within a short period.

Wood View Laundry Walkley. Look how young the girls are.

79A Fred Harrison, wholesale grocer.

Queing at the Castle House Co-op. For the grand opening of the new branch. The Brightside and Carbrook Co-operative Society was formed in 1868. In 1914 it purchased land on Exchange Street for a central stores and offices although due to the First World War it was not begun until 1927, at which point the remains of Sheffield Castle were discovered as the foundations were dug. It was finally completed in 1938 only to be destroyed in the Sheffield Blitz of 13th December 1940. Sheffield Corporation compulsorily purchased the site and the Co-op moved to the Angel Street/Castle Street corner.

Joseph Tomlinson & Sons, funeral directors. Coach and Four outside their premises at Borough Mews in Bedford Street; note the bugler at the back of the coach.

Joseph Tomlinson's charabanc with a full complement of passengers. The vehicle was involved in a nasty crash on the 25th August 1907. It was returning to Sheffield after a tour in Derbyshire, when on passing a horse and trap its wheel hit a telegraph pole which caused it to skid into a stone wall and overturn. Three people were killed in the accident and five others severely injured, one of whom is known to have died of her injuries later. This photograph shows the charabanc after it was rebuilt. How many of these passengers knew of its history?

Prominent Buildings

Fitzalan Square was laid out in 1881 when Market Street and its buildings were demolished; the early square had a substantial cab stand and clock. However, in 1913 this made way for a bronze statue of King Edward VII. The square gets its name from the Fitzalan Market Hall, which stood near the site from 1786 to 1930. The Fitzalans were a branch of the Howard family, Dukes of Norfolk, and the significant local landowners at that time. One of the features of the square is the Grade II listed White Building built in 1908 and faced in faience with carvings of the Sheffield metal trades; the point of the faience was to resist the soot that blackened many of Sheffield's buildings at the time.

Corn Exchange, Broad Street and the new Market Hotel in the 1900s. Sheffield's Corn Exchange was built for the Duke of Norfolk in 1881. Built on a site originally occupied by the Shrewsbury Hospital, at a cost of £55,000, the new Corn Exchange was described by a local newspaper as "one of the greatest architectural beauties of the Town". The Central Hall was gutted by fire in 1947 and the offices surrounding it were demolished in 1964.

The Albert Hall stood in Barker's Pool on the corner of Burgess Street. It was built on the site of the former Quaglen's Circus and opened as a concert hall on 15th December 1873. The interior was described as 'opulent, with fine panels, rich tracery carving and intricate designs of cornucopia and Doric columns'. The hall was used for many different things including concerts, operas, brass band competitions, minstrel and variety shows and magic lantern shows.

Carver Street Methodist Chapel, originally the Wesleyan Methodist Chapel, was built in 1804. In 1873 it had seating for 1300; a rear extension was added at an unknown date. In 1940 the chapel seated 1100 in pews. There was one schoolroom and 20 other rooms. When it was built, the chapel was surrounded by cornfields, known as Cadman's Fields. Few non-conformist chapels in the city had their own burial grounds, but the Carver Street Chapel was an exception. About 1,600 burials took place here between 1805-1855, the gravestones sited in a small front graveyard and on both sides of the building.

Snig Hill looking towards the Pack Horse Inn in West Bar. In 1900 it was decided that Snig Hill would be widened and all the buildings in this photograph were marked for demolition. Bills on the shop closest to the camera advertise an auction of stock that took place on the 3rd and 4th of June 1900, probably not long before this photograph was taken. Other bills advertise the nearby Grand Theatre of Varieties and its music hall acts.

In the short period between the last photograph and 1903 when the properties in Snig Hill demolished new business moved in. As seen in this photo, these included H.H. Schofield, and the London and New Zealand Frozen Mutton Company that had relocated from 50 West Bar. Snig Hill probably gets its name from the wedges that were put behind the horse carts wheels when they stopped on hills, to stop them rolling backwards.

The University of Sheffield received its royal charter in 1905 as successor to the University College of Sheffield, which was established in 1897 by the merger of Sheffield Medical School (founded in 1828), Firth College (1879) and Sheffield Technical School (1884). Steelworkers, coal miners, factory workers and the people of Sheffield donated over £50,000 in 1904 to help found the University. Sheffield is one of the six red brick universities, the civic universities founded in the major industrial cities of England. In 1905, there were 114 full-time students. During the First World War, some of the courses were replaced by teaching munitions making and medical appliances production.

Firth College was founded by Mark Firth (1819 –1880), a local philanthropist and steel manufacturer, to teach arts and science subjects. It then helped to fund the opening of the Sheffield Technical School in 1884 to teach applied science, the only major faculty the existing colleges did not cover. By 1852 Thomas Firth & Sons had expanded into larger premises at the Norfolk Works in Savile Street, which had the largest rolling mill in Sheffield. Sales of file and edge tools to Russia dropped off in the Crimean War, so Firths increased American sales, secured orders for crinoline hoops, then switched to armaments, specializing in gun tubes and projectiles. By 1860 Armstrongs, Vavasseurs, and Woolwich Arsenal were major customers.

Hunter's Bar is a former toll bar on Ecclesall Road active until the late 19th century which now stands in the middle of the roundabout. The gatekeeper for the toll bar lived in a house on the corner of Ecclesall Road and Sharrow Vale Road. The area is featured in the Arctic Monkeys' song *Fake Tales of San Francisco*, in particular the lyric, "*He talks of San Francisco, he's from Hunter's Bar*". Hunter's Bar roundabout has its own Twitter account and its own website.

The Sheffield Botanical Gardens is off Ecclesall Road and can boast 5,000 species of plants in 19 acres. The gardens opened in 1836 with the most notable features being the Grade II* listed glass pavilions, restored and reopened in 2003. Other notable structures are the main gateway, the south entrance lodge and a bear pit. The Sheffield Botanical and Horticultural Society was formed in 1833 and by 1834 had obtained £7,500 in funding leading to the purchase of 18 acres from the estate of local snuff manufacturer Joseph Wilson.

The magnificent Cutlers' Hall in Church Street is the headquarters of the Company of Cutlers in Hallamshire. It was built in 1832 and is Sheffield's third Cutlers' Hall; the previous buildings on the same site, were constructed in 1638 and 1725. As might be expected the hall can boast some spectacular exhibits including a selection of old Hallamshire knives, some of which go back to the Elizabethan era. Many of the knives were discovered by Thames mud-larks. Then there is the Norfolk Knife, a huge pocket knife with 75 blades made by Joseph Rodgers and Sons at their Norfolk Street Works for the Crystal Palace Great Exhibition of 1851. The earliest building was used for the Cutlers' Feast which became an annual event in 1648. By 2008, there had been 372 Cutlers' Feasts, with breaks only for the World Wars and a cancellation in 1921.

A mosaic in the floor of the hall.

A view along Wicker from the River Don. The road is famed for its history and the viaduct that crosses it, the Grade II* listed Wicker Arches which can be seen in the distance. An early reference to the Wicker comes from the records of the Sheffield Town Trust for 1572: 'Item, payd to William Dyker for mending of the Butt in the Wycker', and earlier the same year: 'Item, paid to William Dyker and Johne Greave for makinge the nare butt in the Sembley grene'.

Tinsley's Carnegie library opened in June 1905, a few months before Walkley's, and seven years before Tinsley, then an independent township, became part of Sheffield. It served as the branch library until 1985 and was financed by the Scottish-American steel magnate and philanthropist Andrew Carnegie.

Hillsborough Barracks is a walled complex of buildings between Langsett Road and Penistone Road, comprising 22 acres, dating from 1848 and replacing the barracks at Hillfoot. Hillsborough was, to a large extent, self-contained: it was divided into three terraces. The first (top) terrace contained the Mess, quarters for around 40 officers and a similar number of servants, and a chapel. The other buildings consisted of a large five-bedroomed house serving as the Garrison Commander's Quarters outside the walls, a 58-patient two-storey hospital incorporating barracks for RAMC personnel, a dental clinic and 'a facility for treating women', infantry soldiers' quarters, a clock tower building, with cavalry soldiers' quarters on the first floor and stabling for 260 horses on the ground floor, accommodation for 918 NCO and other ranks. The last Army unit, the 29th Field (Howitzer) Battery, left the Barracks in February 1930.

A group of Royal Engineers, at Hillsborough Barracks 19th May 1916.

Grade II* listed building Park Hill (the largest listed building in Europe) is a Brutalist syle social housing estate built between 1957 and 1961. It was built on the site of back-to-back housing, 2–3-storey tenement buildings, waste ground and quarries. There were shared privies that were not connected to mains drainage with one standpipe catering for up to 100 people. Due to the high rates of violent crime it was known as "Little Chicago". Clearance began during the 1930s. The 995 Park Hill flats and maisonettes, 3 pubs and 31 shops were built in 4 street decks, wide enough for milk floats, linked by bridges across the upper decks; the flats were described as streets in the sky.

The Music Hall in Sheffield, on Surrey Street around 1830, was the main concert and meeting hall and venue for art exhibitions in the city during much of the 19th century. The medical school can be seen on the right. From *The History of the City of Sheffield 1843-1993: Images*.

The New Athenaeum and Mechanics' Institute in Sheffield on Surrey Street circa 1850 from *The History of the City of Sheffield 1843-1993: Images*. The Sheffield Mechanics' Institute was founded in 1832. Before 1847 it occupied a site on Surrey Street, on or adjacent to where the present-day central library stands. It was decided to build new premises, on the other side of Surrey Street somewhat contentiously and confusingly this was to house a club, the "Athenaeum" and the existing Mechanics' Institute. The foundation stone of the new building was laid on 1st September 1847. This was distinct from the pre-existing Sheffield Athenaeum Club in Norfolk Street. From the beginning, the combination of the two elements caused conflict, so in 1851 they severed their connection, though they continued to occupy the same building. The Mechanics section reverted to being called Sheffield Mechanics Institution but since there was, as noted, already a Sheffield Athenaeum Club, the Athenaeum section became the Sheffield Lyceum Club. This is the layout of the Institute: three stories, lowest rented by the Corporation (Free Library); second floor, Lecture Hall; top floor used by students of the Institute, reportedly "inconvenient".

Above: The Sheffield Telegraph in 1898. *The Sheffield Telegraph* was founded in 1855 as the *Sheffield Daily Telegraph*; it was the city's first daily newspaper with an aim to popularise the Conservative Party among the working class. By 1898, it had sales of 1,250,000 copies per week.

Left: The composing room, not that very long ago. This is how newspaper pages used to be made up. No photoshop or cut and paste here.

Dial House is a Grade II listed building on Ben Lane; it was originally a small country house, before becoming a working men's club. The vertical sundial bears the date 1802 and the name Coopland on it. Coopland may have been the first family to live in the house or were the makers of the sundial.

The Debtors' Gaol, Scotland Street, Eccleshall. A letter dated 7th July, 1825 from the Home Office enquired *"whether [there] is any Prison at Ecclesall, and if so, what is the nature of it, and the number of Prisoners it is capable of containing."* The Rev: Matthew Preston, the minister of Ecclesall Chapel, replied on the 13th July, 1825, stating there was in the chapelry a *"jail for the confinement of debtors committed in execution for small debts under £5 for the manor of Ecclesall"* and he proceeded to give details which he obtained from the bailiff: *"Demensions of Ecclesall Court House, and Prison: One Court Room to hear and determine Causes Amounting to Five Pounds, seven yards by eight yards long. One Room to receive and pay money therein, four yards by four. Three Rooms underneath the Court house as prison for debtors capable of containing fourteen Prisoners, one of which is six yards by seven, the other two is three yards by seven. The yard for the Prisoners to walk is thirty five yards round. There is one Pump in the yd. which is oft dry in the summer season. The Gaoler house contains two low rooms and three chambers, the above is the Property of Earl Fitzwilliam, Lord of the Manor of Ecclesall in the County of York"*.

Some rules:
Rule 9. *"No person is allowed to play at cards during meal times, nor before seven in the morning, nor after eleven at night, unless agreeable to the whole room, or forfeit one shilling; and any prisoner giving false notice, to forfeit one shilling."*
Rule 20. *"If there be any familiarity between man and wife, and another prisoner make mention of the same, he shall be fined one shilling."*

The Blitz and the Second World War

Sheffield endured sixteen raids during The Second World War causing 631 deaths and injuring 1,817. The first bomb fell on the night of August 18th 1940; the last on July 28th 1942. There were 130 alerts. The Sheffield Blitz refers to two raids, on the nights of 12th December and 15th December 1940. The night of Thursday 12th December 1940 was particularly bad for Sheffield when 280 German bombers raided. Their target was the steel works producing armaments in the east end of the city, but an all too frequent error in navigation and bomb aiming meant that the city centre was to become the main target. Fire bombs caused widespread panic and wholesale destruction. Sheffield with its heavy industry, much of which was repurposed for war work and armaments, was an obvious target. Documents seized at the end of the war showed that the targets for the raids included the Atlas Steelworks, Brown Bayley Steelworks, Meadowhall Iron Works, River Don Works, Darnall Wagon Works, Tinsley Park Collieries, East Hecla Works and Orgreave Coke Ovens. The full moon was on 14th December 1940 and both blitz nights were cold and reasonably clear. Fittingly, the German code name for the operation was Schmelztiegel, "Crucible".

(This file is licensed under the Creative Commons Attribution-Share Alike 4.0 International license. Chemical Engineer.)

Hadfields Limited of Hecla and East Hecla, Sheffield, was a British manufacturer of special steels, in particular manganese alloys which were discovered by the founder's son in 1882 and often known as Hadfield steel and the manufacture of steel castings. Robert Hadfield (1858–1940) also invented silicon steel. By the time of his death in 1888 it was estimated there were more than 1,500,000 Hadfield's cast steel wheels and axles in daily use all over the world and his firm could make castings weighing up to 16,000 lb (7 ton); he was able to produce cast steel of a strength previously provided only by forged steel. The company was heavily involved in the armaments industry, turning out shells and armour plate steel and the only firm in the UK at that time making 18-inch armour-piercing shells (pictured left, at Kelham Island Museum). Although only 500 were made between 1916 and 1919. Hadfield could produce materials and castings for shells which previously had to be imported from France. By 1911 Hadfield's was believed to employ more workmen than any other business in Sheffield and was "largely engaged in the production of war material." Their 14 in (356 mm) Heclon armour piercing shot weighing almost 1,700 lb could perforate 12 in of Krupp cemented armour plate without shattering. Hadfield's shells had a patent cap which gave their projectiles very high ballistic qualities. Their Era cast steel was used in the armoured structures in warships.

The attack was made by three main groups of aircraft flying from airfields in northern France. Thirteen Heinkel 111s from Kampfgruppe 100, the German Pathfinder unit arrived over the city at 7:41 pm and dropped 16 SC50 high-explosive bombs, 1,009 B1 E1 ZA incendiaries and 10,080 B1 E1 incendiaries. The first incendiaries landed on Norton Lees and Gleadless. The first main group was made up of three waves of 36 Junkers 88s and 29 Heinkel 111s. The second group comprised 23 Junkers 88s, 74 Heinkel 111s and seven Dornier 17s. The last group was made up of 63 Junkers 88s and 35 Heinkel 111s, a total of 280 aircraft. At about 9:30 pm a stick of bombs fell on Campo Lane and Vicar Lane, demolishing the west end of the cathedral. Most of the 450 HE bombs and six parachute mines bombs fell on the city centre or on residential districts with the last bombs falling at 4 am. Fourteen tramcars were destroyed during the blitz while six employees were killed and fourteen were injured while at work.

The building at the corner of Fitzalan Square where it joins High Street was occupied during the 1870s by the Wine and Spirit Commercial Hotel. By the late 1880s it was known as Market Street Wine Vaults; John Marples became the proprietor in 1886 and called it the London Mart, but it was always known locally as "The Marples". During the raid of December 12th lots of people took shelter in the Marples' extensive cellars, feeling that they would be they safe with the protection afforded by the robust seven-storey building above them. At 10.50 p.m. C&A

Modes department store opposite Marples on High Street took a direct hit from a 500 kg bomb. Flying debris from the explosion hurtled into the Marples pub, the cellar bar known as the 'Tudor Lounge', injuring a number of customers who were taken down into the cellars, some into the 'Bottle Stores' next to the cellar bar where they remained with five other men. At 11.44 p.m. the Marples building took a direct hit from a bomb which plunged right through the building and detonated just above the cellars, killing approximately 70 people and reducing the building to a 15-foot-high pile of rubble and human remains. The next day seven men were dug out of the rubble still alive, as a small section of cellar roof had, incredibly, withstood the impact; two of them walked away from the scene unaided although one, from Pomona Street later committed suicide in 1943. Allegedly the roofs of the cellars in the London Mart were not strengthened; the survivors were apparently in that smaller bottling cellar that had a stronger ceiling.

Over the next few weeks 64 bodies were recovered and the partial remains of six or seven other people. All but six were from Sheffield. The force of the explosion and the collapse of the building meant that only 14 people could be visually identified: the remainder were identified by their personal belongings. Nine other pubs were destroyed

that night: The Westminster – High Street; The Royal Oak – King Street; The Devonshire Arms – South Street, The Moor; The Shades Vaults – Watson's Walk (founded in 1797);The Three Horse Shoes – Norfolk Street (Jehu Street); The Kings Head – 1 Change Alley (1772); The Angel – 15 Angel Street (1657). Other pubs were badly damaged, including the Cossack at the foot of Howard Street next to Sheffield Hallam University's City Campus; its top floor and roof blown were off in the raid and it has been a single storey "bungalow pub." ever since.

The second night of the Blitz on the 15th of December saw the first deployment of a new Luftwaffe policy for their pathfinders. High-explosive bombs were replaced by incendiaries. The pathfinder force was made up of 16 Heinkel 111s that dropped 11,520 B1 E1 incendiaries between 7 pm and 7:50 pm. The resultant 15 large fires and the numerous small fires were visible from 100 miles away. The main raid was carried out by 50 Heinkel 111s and 11 Dornier 17s. The raid finished at 10:15 pm. Many steelworks received hits, including Hadfields, Brown Bayleys and Steel, Peech and Tozer Ltd, although the damage failed to affect production.

Repairing tram tracks in Fitzalan Square after the bombing. In total the Blitz claimed 660 people, 1,500 injured and 40,000 were made homeless. 3,000 homes were demolished with a further 3,000 badly damaged. A total of 78,000 homes had some damage. Six George Medals were awarded to citizens of Sheffield for their bravery during the raids. 134 victims were buried in a communal grave in City Road Cemetery.

German Messerschmitt 109 shot down at Margate on display in Burgess Street? Barker's Pool. The Messerschmitt Bf 109-E4 "White 5" of the JG 53 "Ace of Spades" squadron was brought back to Sheffield and put on display in Barker's Pool as a war trophy to boost morale and raise money for the Sheffield Newspapers War Fund, "Salute the Airmen" – a fundraising effort where you could buy a sticker and stick it on the aircraft. It was shot down over Margate, Kent on 6th September 1940. The pilot was Unteroffizier Hans-Georg Schulte who took off at 17.30 hrs on a freelance patrol and was flying with four other Bf 109's at 16,500 ft when shot down by British fighters at 18.50 hrs. The pilot tried to land at Manston Aerodrome, but crashed near Vincents Farm, Manston at 18.30hrs. Schulte was credited with eight air-to-air combat victories including two Spitfires and two Hurricanes; the eighth and final one was a Spitfire, probably shot down immediately before he was himself forced to land at Vincents Farm: Note that the swastika on the tail fin has been painted out. That was reportedly because the squadron Wing Commander, Hans-Jürgen Erdmann von Cramon-Taubadel, married a girl who was 'not suitable', ie she was Jewish. He therefore was ordered to remove the squadron's "Ace of Spades" mascot from the cowlings of their Messerschmitts and paint a red band around the noses of their aircraft as a mark of shame. When Cramon-Taubadel was replaced, the "Ace of Spades" mascot was reinstated, but, in response to this, the unit over-painted the swastikas of their aircraft in protest. Much of this fascinating story, and the following related image, come from a post by Sheffield History member, dr_gn February 24, 2010: www.sheffieldhistory.co.uk.

Unteroffizier Hans-Georg Schulte. Schulte is second from the left, looking at the camera. His aircraft "White 5" is in the background.

Barrage balloon girls at Petre Street barrage balloon site 23rd July 1940. Sheffield's barrage balloon history goes back to before the Second World War when an auxiliary squadron was set up. Commanders were selected from the First World War veterans who volunteered to accept a commission and help out with the training, organising and establishment of this new defensive force. No. 33 Group Royal Air Force set up No.16 Balloon Centre in Sheffield. In March 1939 Captain R. Caley M.C. accepted a commission as a Squadron Leader and was put in command of 939 Squadron (West Riding) and was the very first Royal Auxiliary Air Force officer to serve in Sheffield – as 90652 Squadron Leader Caley. It had been decided that the men required for balloon work were to be of a medical grade that would have rejected them for normal service and an age limit for Airmen of 32 to 50, with N.C.O.'s age 55; officers 32 to 50 years of age. Over 1,000 Sheffield people volunteered to serve in the balloons.

Barrage balloon on Crookesmoor Recreation ground. 192466 Wing Commander Ralph Eric Maxwell Cherry M.C was selected as Commanding Officer of Sheffield's No.16 Balloon Centre and the three Auxiliary Air Force squadrons attached to it were all based at 641 Attercliffe Road before moving to a site at Lightwood. No.16 Balloon Centre had three squadrons: 939 Squadron (West Riding) with 40 balloons at Sheffield; 940 Squadron (West Riding), with headquarters at the Station Hotel, Rotherham with 32 balloons and 941 Squadron (Central) with headquarters at Scott Road, Osgathorpe – disbanded in 1941. WAAFs were not initially selected to fly balloons but a trial to see if women crews could "man" balloons successfully was carried out at No.16 Balloon Centre in July 1941: eight WAAF crews were formed comprising around 324 women with 16 women instead of 11 men proving that they could adequately fly a balloon. This marked the start of Sheffield becoming a centre of excellence for the training of women in balloons and allowed men to be sent elsewhere for other vital tasks. It was, however, seen in some quarters as a humiliation to men. Much of this is abridged from *Barrage Balloons Protecting Sheffield Before and During The War* by peter.garwood@bbrclub.org. Balloon Barrage Reunion Club.

A.R.P. Ambulance Station and crews on Ecclesall Rd. In April 1937 the government had asked for Air Raid Precautions (ARP) to be set up across the country. These precautions included Air Raid Wardens, casualty services, First Aid posts and Emergency Feeding and Rest Centres, amongst other things. The women of the ARP provided care, supported the homeless, helped children to trace missing parents, and provided comfort for people who needed it. During the Blitz the headquarters suffered three direct hits and over 75% of the Emergency Feeding and Rest centres were rendered inoperable.

Women of Steel is an impressive, award-winning bronze sculpture that commemorates the dignified and inspirational women of Sheffield who worked in the city's steel industry during the World Wars; it was sculpted by Martin Jennings and unveiled in June 2016. Additional money that was raised for the statue in the fundraising appeal paid for medallions to commemorate the women made by the Sheffield Assay Office, with 100 women having applied for them as well as 400 family members of deceased women steelworkers.

Right: On 8th May 1945 Nazi Germany signed the definitive version of its unconditional surrender, marking the end of the Second World War in Europe. Even before the surrender, in the autumn of 1944, the day was called VE Day in anticipation of Victory in Europe, and celebrations were planned for whenever the final victory would be. Like these celebrations in Rushdale Avenue. Note the effigy of Hitler.

Below: After Victory in Europe came Victory in Japan or VJ Day, which in the UK was taken as the moment Japan made its initial announcement of surrender on 15th August 1945. The document was signed on 2nd of September, on the deck of the USS *Missouri* in Tokyo Bay, which is recognised as VJ Day (or VP Day for Pacific) in the USA. Again it was a cause for celebration, like this VJ Day street party.

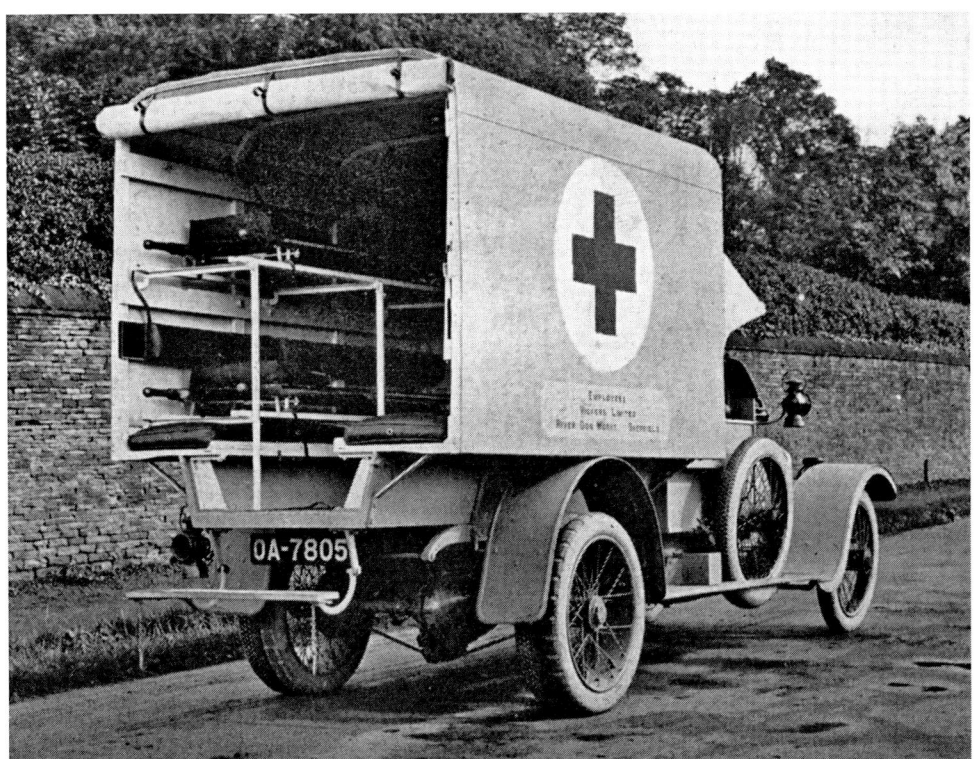

Left: Ambulance presented to the British Red Cross Society by the Vickers' Employees War Relief Fund, Sheffield, 14th August 1915.

Below: This ambulance was presented as a joint gift by the members of the Sheffield and Ecclesall and Brightside and Carbrook Co-operative Societies, 4th November, 1915. Cost £556.

The first ever motorised ambulances to transport wounded people were used in the First World War. Before that motor ambulances had never been used in war, they cost money. The wounded men of 1914 were therefore shaken and rocked in horse-drawn ambulance wagons and lumbering motor wagons. Journeys were agonising, especially over the stoney roads of northern France. On 12 September 1914, a small meeting was held at the Royal Automobile Club, at which a few members offered to place themselves and their cars at the disposal of the Red Cross. The Red Cross established the motor ambulance department, which sent 3,446 motor vehicles, including 2171 motor ambulances, to various destinations throughout the war. In total, 94 ambulances were destroyed by the enemy and subsequently scrapped by the Joint WarCommittee.

Six tanks toured England in late 1917-late 1918. Tank No. 30 was called *Nelson*. It left Sheffield on 16th December to go to Bristol. The tanks were transported by rail; initially they were loaded on 'ordinary' low loaders, driving on from a ramp at the rear. Later specially designed tank transporter railway wagons were used – these allowed side load driving on from a parallel platform. War bonds are debt securities issued by a government to finance military operations and other expenditure in times of war. In practice, governments finance war by injecting additional money into circulation, and the function of the bonds is to remove that money from circulation and help to control inflation. War bonds are either retail bonds marketed directly to the public or wholesale bonds traded on a stock market.

Light reconnaisance cars of the Sheffield Home Guard, Blonk St. 1940.

Hospitals

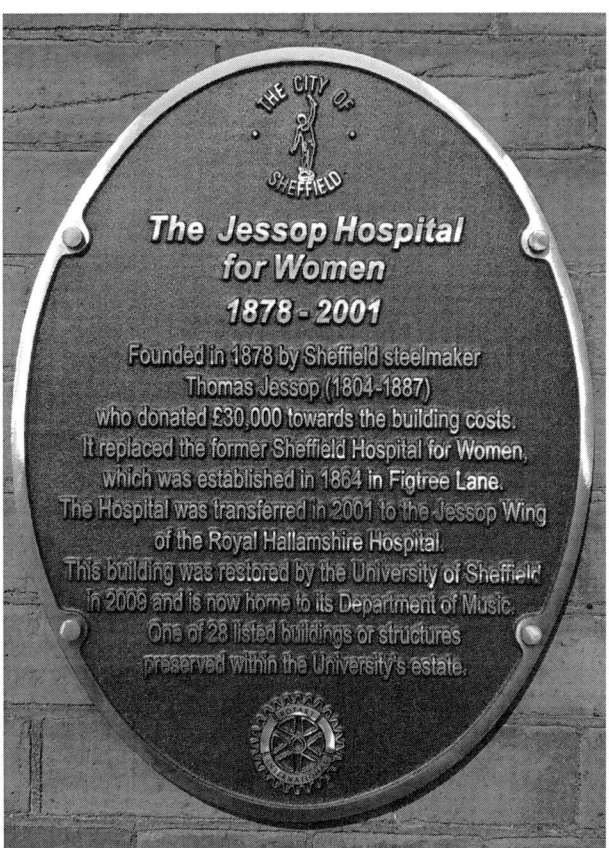

Jessop Hospital for Sick Women, in Figtree Lane was founded by three local doctors. Having only six beds, later extended to nine, it soon outgrew the building, so a site was found in Levygreave and, in 1875, Thomas Jessop provided the funds to buy it and build the Jessop; it could accommodate 57 in-patients and cater for out-patients. Extensions were made in 1902 and 1918 and by 1920 the Diseases of Women Department provided 64 beds, the Maternity Department 28 beds and there were 25 cots. An extension, the Edwardian wing, was completed in 1902. Between 1927 and 1972 the hospital had a 45 bed annexe at Norton Hall known as the Firth Auxiliary Hospital; it could house 45 antenatal and fever cases. The main hospital was badly damaged in an air raid in 1940 and new buildings were completed in 1943. By 1948 there were 211 beds including 47 at the Firth where there was a special provision for the treatment of puerperal sepsis in an open air ward. The Jessop closed in 2001.

The Third Northern General Hospital, December has its origins in the Fir Vale workhouse and 1878 infirmary. When it opened in September 1881 the infirmary block had capacity for 366 patients; a ward for treating women with venereal diseases was established in the 1890s. The infirmary block was re-built and became the Sheffield Union Hospital when the workhouse was renamed the Fir Vale Institution in 1906. The Sheffield Union Hospital became the Fir Vale Hospital and the Fir Vale Institution became Fir Vale House a few years later. In 1930 the Fir Vale Hospital became the City General Hospital and Fir Vale House became the Fir Vale Infirmary. Confused? The City General Hospital performed the world's first heart valve replacement operation in 1955. 'This particular set of photographs is taken from a collection held at Tyne & Wear Archives capturing the everyday lives of the nurses and patients at the 3rd Northern General Hospital, Sheffield and Longshaw Lodge Convalescent Home for Wounded Soldiers, Grindleford, near Sheffield. The photographs were taken between August 1916 and June 1917. Provided within the spirit of The Commons. 'Tyne & Wear Archives & Museums'.

'Shrewsbury Hospital, Sheffield, Yorkshire'. Engraving by John Rogers after Nathaniel Whittock (1791–1860). This file comes from Wellcome Images, a website operated by the Wellcome Trust. The original Shrewsbury Hospital was a row of almshouses and a chapel. Gilbert Talbot, 13th Earl of Shrewsbury declared in his will that he wanted to found a "hospital" i.e almshouses "at Sheffield for the perpetual maintenance of 20 poor persons." The home for the 20 poor people was built near Sheffield Castle and completed in 1666. These original almshouses became dilapidated and in the early 19th century a new site on Norfolk Road was chosen for the almshouses which were built between 1825 and 1828.

Consumptive patients undergoing treatment at the Royal Infirmary, Sheffield in 1899. The hospital opened as the Sheffield General Infirmary in 1792. It was renamed The Royal Infirmary, Sheffield in 1897. The photograph is from *The Consumptive Working Man : what can sanatoria do for him?* by N.D. Bardswell, London: Scientific Press (1906).

Crookes

Crookes can be found near the course of a Roman road from Templeborough to Brough-on-Noe; the main road is itself over 1,000 years old. Founded by the Vikings as 'Krkur' in AD 980, the area was recorded in the Doomsday Boo kas "Crokkiss". Crookes was a self-contained village from the 16th century until the end of the 19th century. It was sparsely settled until the 1790s, when a turnpike road was opened from Sheffield to Glossop.

Crookes about 1905.

The Great Sheffield Flood

The Great Sheffield Flood laid waste parts of Sheffield on 11th March 1864, when the Dale Dyke Dam gave way just as its 76 acre reservoir was filling up for the first time. The view looks up-valley with the ruptured dam in the foreground, and the little water that was left in the reservoir behind it. The dam was in Bradfield Dale near Low Bradfield on the River Loxley. The immediate cause was a crack in the embankment, but the source of the crack was never determined. The dam was rebuilt in 1875. Rapid industrialization led to Sheffield's population mushrooming from 45,478 in 1801 to 185,157 in 1861. One consequence was a greatly increased demand for water: the construction of the Dale Dyke Dam was part of the plan to provide a more efficient source of clean water and was created by the Sheffield Waterworks Company who in the late 1850s bought land in the Loxley Valley to the north-west of the town on which to build a reservoir. By the 1860s the dam had been signed off as satisfactory and filling went ahead. On that fateful night in March 1864 an estimated 700 million gallons of water cascaded down the Loxley Valley, through Loxley Village and on to Malin Bridge and Hillsborough, at the confluence of the Rivers Loxley and River Don. The torrent continued south down the Don into Sheffield centre, around the eastward bend of the Don at Lady's Bridge, then to Attercliffe, past the sites of what later became Don Valley Stadium, Sheffield Arena and Meadowhall Centre, and on to Rotherham. At the Hillsborough Barracks the flood waters breached a stone wall that was three feet thick. The water rose to the height of twelve feet outside the window of Sergeant Foulds' quarters and drowned two of his children.

Tragically 238 people died and some 700 animals were drowned; 415 dwelling houses, 106 factories and shops and 64 other buildings were wrecked and 500 partially damaged; 15 bridges were swept away and six others badly damaged. http://mick-armitage.staff.shef.ac.uk/sheffield/flood.html gives us more detail: 'The youngest to drown was a two-day-old baby boy, the oldest a woman of eighty-seven. Whole families were wiped out; one man, trapped upstairs in a terrace house, battered his way through five party walls to safety collecting thirty-four other people as he went; a would be suicide, locked in a cell, decided, as the flood poured in, that he no longer wished to die… a husband put his wife and five children on a bed on which they floated until the water went down.' After about thirty minutes the flood gradually subsided leaving a trail of destruction more than eight miles long: it was later described as 'looking like a battlefield'. Claims for damages formed one of the largest insurance claims of the Victorian period. The Government started a Board of Inundation Commissioners to pass judgement for compensation claims against the Waterworks Company. They also arbitrated 7,500 claims for loss of life and property which totalled £455,000. All but 650 claims were settled without recourse to the arbitration process, but those 650 claims took almost six months to process. The claims registers record the claimant, their marital status and address, as well as details of the claim and the outcome, and amount awarded in compensation. As such they provide a unique insight into mid-Victorian Sheffield's trade and industry with claims listed for shop and factory stock, tools and premises damaged and lost. The domestic claims for furniture, clothes, books, toys and household utensils and goods help build up an unrivalled picture of workers' lives at the time. For more fascinating details see https://www2.shu.ac.uk/sfca/#. The catastrophe resulted in reforms in engineering practice, setting rigorous standards that had to be met when constructing such large-scale structures.

Talking about Sheffield

Ther was no man, for peril, dorste hym touche. A Sheffeld thwitel baar he in his hose. Round was his face, and camus was his nose;
    Geoffrey Chaucer, "The Reeve's Tale", in *The Canterbury Tales*, (1297)

It is a pretty long Parish and through it runs a water which came down a great banck at the end of town…they say it runs off of a poisonous mine or soile and from Coale pitts, they permit none to taste it, for I sent for a Cup of it and the people in the Street call'd out to forbid the tasteing it.
    Celia Fiennes, *Through England On a Side Saddle: in the Time of William and Mary*, (1888)

This town of Sheffield is very populous and large, the streets narrow, and the houses dark and black, occasioned by the continued smoke of the forges, which are always at work: Here they make all sorts of cutlery-ware, but especially that of edged-tools, knives, razors, axes, &. and nails.
    Daniel Defoe, *A Tour Through the Whole Island of Great Britain* (1724).

Some houses are brick, some stone, and there is a fair number of pretty ones; but they are lost in such a multitude of shapeless huts and outlandish factory-buildings that Sheffield could never pass for a fine town.
    Alexandre and François La Rochefoucauld, diaries, translation by Norman Scarfe, *Innocent Espionage: The LA Rochefoucauld Brothers' Tour of England* in 1785

If the people of Sheffield could only receive a tenth part of what their knives sell for by retail in America, Sheffield might pave its streets with silver.
William Cobbett, *Rural Rides*, (1830).

Generally in Sheffield the average of the comfort of the lower classes is above that of most other places; we have not yet got into the abominable way of cellars or of many families living in the same house.
    John Parker, Parliamentary Select Committee on Public Walks: *Minutes of Evidence* (1833), quoted in Clyde Binfield et al, *The History of the City of Sheffield 1843-1993: Volume One: Politics*, (1993).

What a beautiful place Sheffield would be, if Sheffield were not there!
    Walter White, *A Month in Yorkshire*, (1861).

ONE beauty of Sheffield is that you can see very little of it at a time… Beyond, in every direction, is a screen of torpid smoke which obscures the sky, and tones the warm radiance behind it to a mellow and sometimes golden twilight. Out of the clinging folds countless slender chimneys immensely high streak the monotonous color that surrounds them, and from each issues a woolly black stream that, lacking the natural buoyancy and diffusiveness of smoke, seems to clot in the sultry air.
Description of Sheffield in an article by William Rideing, an American author, published in *Harper's Magazine* in 1884.

There is no more public spirit in Sheffield than there is in the smallest village of Yorkshire.
    Thomas Moore, *Sheffield Independent*, 16th April 1870, quoted in Clyde Binfield et al, *The History of the City of Sheffield 1843-1993: Volume One: Politics*, (1993).

I see a pretty state of things in your Municipality. Everything is mean, petty, and narrow in the extreme. What a contrast to Leeds!
    Anthony John Mundella, letter of October 1871 to Robert Leader, quoted in Clyde Binfield et al, *The History of the City of Sheffield 1843-1993: Volume One: Politics*, (1993).

The progress of Sheffield in my lifetime has been something wonderful. Why, in my young days it was a little bit of a place of no consequence and no trade. When I think of the small notions and little minds of the public men of old Sheffield I can hardly realise that the City has become the fine important flourishing place it is today, one of the largest Cities of the Empire.
    Frederick Mappin, 1905, quoted in Sidney Pollard, *A History of Labour in Sheffield*, (1959).

It could justly claim to be called the ugliest town in the Old World: its inhabitants, who want it to be pre-eminent in everything, very likely make that claim for it … And the stench! If at rare moments you stop smelling sulphur it is because you have begun smelling gas.
    George Orwell, *The Road to Wigan Pier* (1937)

When I go back to Sheffield I feel very close to it – although the whole family has moved away, there's something about the people, about the manners that I recognise.
    Margaret Drabble

Architecturally a miserable disappointment.
    Nikolaus Pevsner, *Buildings of England* (1959)